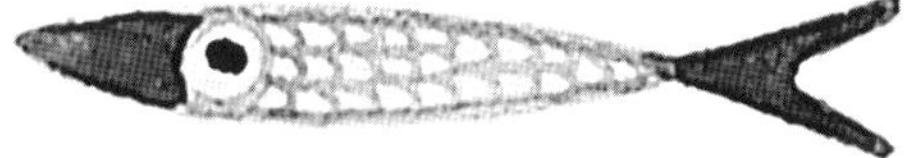

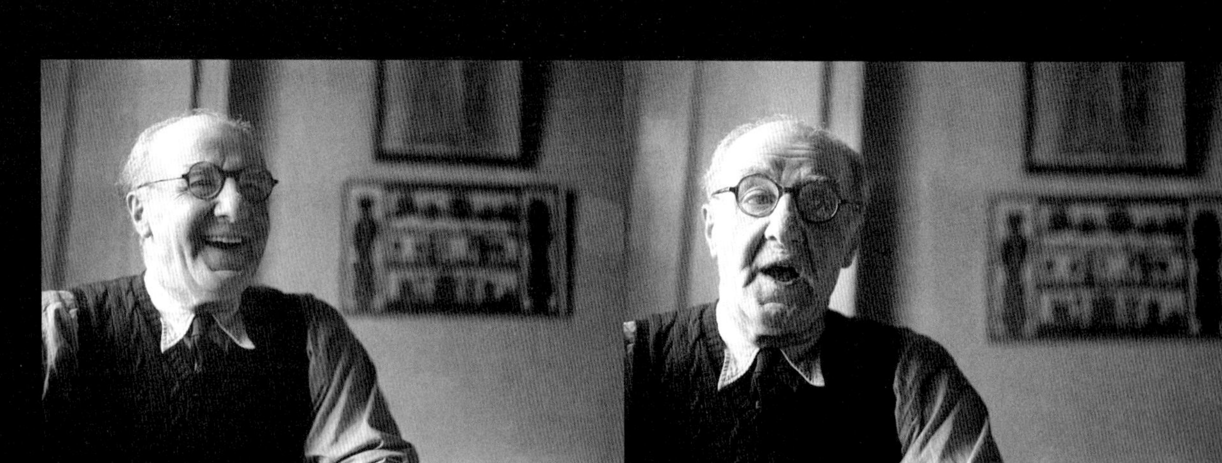

SCOTTIE WILSON
Peddler Turned Painter

ANTHONY J. PETULLO AND KATHERINE M. MURRELL

PETULLO PUBLISHING LLC, MILWAUKEE

COVER:
Detail of *Center Fish Circle on Black*, c. 1965
Colored ink on paper
$14^3/_8$ x $10^7/_8$ inches (36.5 x 27.6 centimeters)
The Anthony Petullo Collection of Self-Taught and Outsider Art

PAGES 2 and 80:
Scottie Wilson
Photographer: Crispin Eurich (1936–76)
© 'The First' Gallery, South Hampton, SO18 5DG, UK.
www.CrispinEurich.com

Published by Petullo Publishing LLC, 312 E. Buffalo Street, Suite 200, Milwaukee, WI 53202

Library of Congress Control Number: 2004090125

ISBN 0-9748740-0-0

Edited by Karen Jacobson

Layout and design by Michelle Pietrzak-Wegner

Artwork photography by Larry Sanders Photography, Milwaukee, Wisconsin,
except for *Textile with Scottie Wilson Design*, courtesy of the V&A Picture Library.

Printed in Canada by Friesens Corporation

Contents

1   Louis Freeman, Peddler · 7

2   The Early Years, 1891–1906 · 9

3   Military Service, 1906–c. 1920 · 13

4   A London Shopkeeper, c. 1922–32 · 17

5   From Peddler to Painter: Canada, 1932–45 · 19

6   Return to Britain, 1945 · 31

7   An "Outsider" Artist in London, 1945–72 · 37

8   Scottie's Legacy · 49

Plates · 33

Chronology · 61

Exhibition History · 63

Bibliography · 69

Acknowledgments · 73

Index · 75

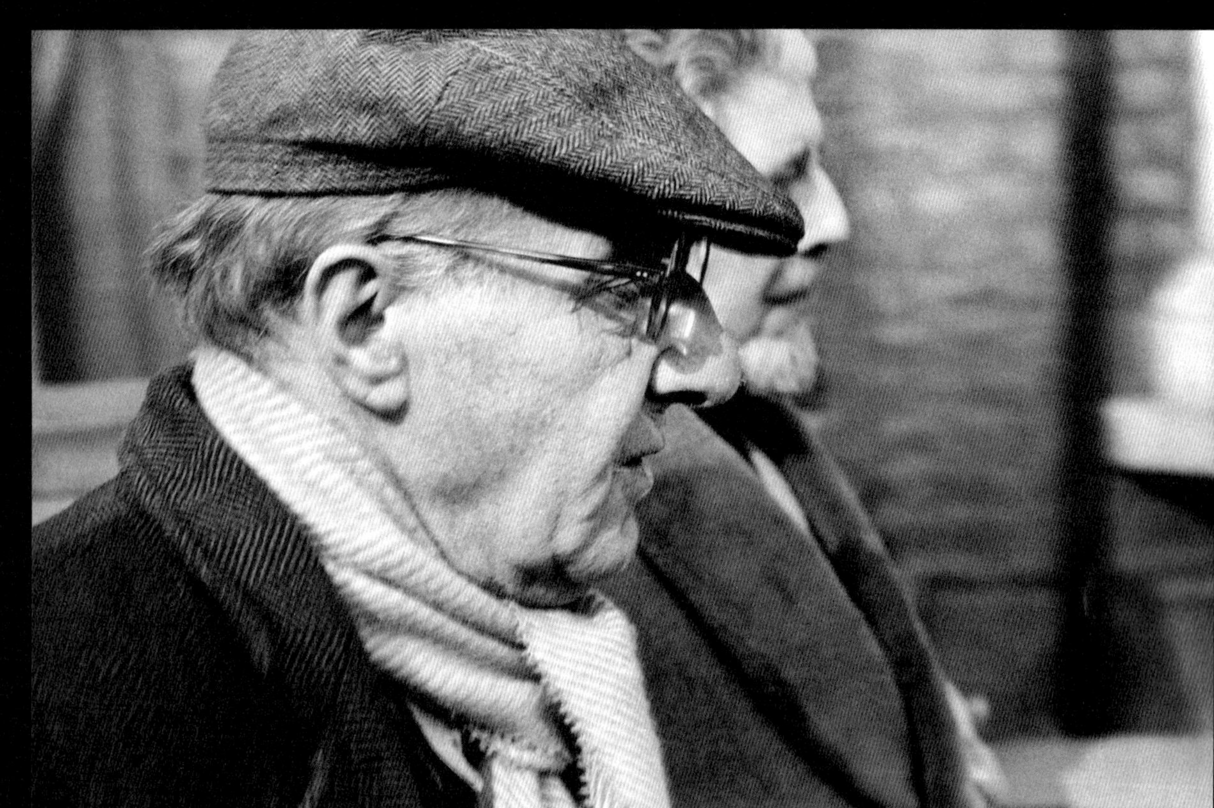

Louis Freeman, Peddler

Louis Freeman was a peddler. He was a loner, elusive and secretive. Very few people knew much about him, and he liked it that way. He was cautious and suspicious and had strong moral convictions. At age forty-one he was an illiterate shopkeeper with a secondhand store in northwest London. And even though he was clever and determined, the odds were against him.

The year was 1932, and the world looked very bleak. The Great Depression had overtaken most nations, and world leaders couldn't agree on how to revitalize the global economy. Disarmament conferences ended in failure. Japan invaded Manchuria. Anti-Semitism was on the rise in Germany, where Hitler would soon become chancellor. Unemployment in major industrial countries had been rising for two years. In the United States it hit a peak of 24 percent—13,000,000 people—and industry was operating at half the 1929 capacity. Conditions in the United Kingdom were almost as harsh. Some 3,750,000 people, 19 percent of a workforce of 20,000,000, were unemployed. Businesses were failing, and jobs were nonexistent. The British economy had collapsed.

Louis Freeman—the sometime shopkeeper, sometime street trader—was very likely finding it difficult to survive. Few people had money to buy what he was selling, and even if businesses had been hiring, he had no other marketable skills. So in 1932 Freeman made a life-changing decision and left for Canada—for the second time. He would later explain to an interviewer that his reason for relocating was an impulse that suddenly struck him "like a kick in the pants."[1] Thirteen years later he would return to England not as a street peddler but as an artist called Robert "Scottie" Wilson. While in Canada he would discover a talent and a passion that would make him an artistic celebrity. He would soon become one of the best-known self-taught artists in Britain, France, and Canada.

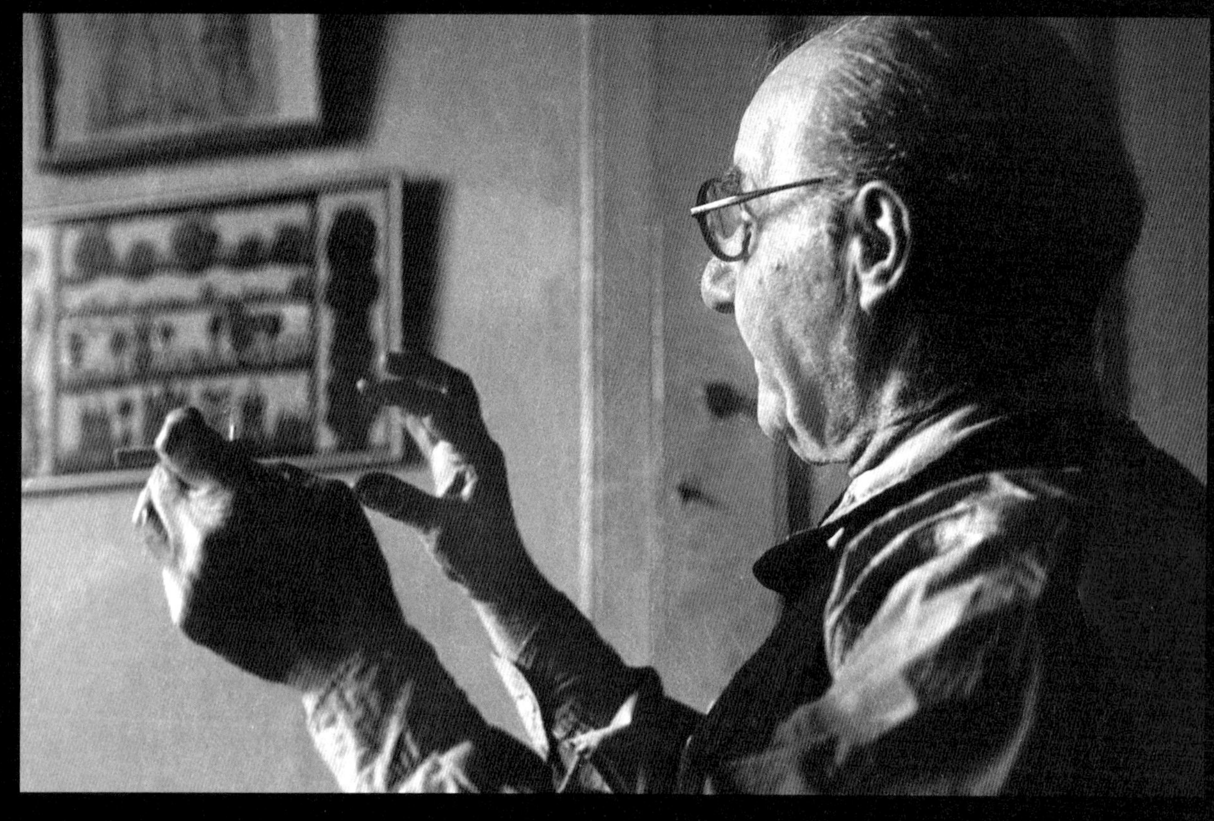

The Early Years, 1891–1906

Scottie Wilson was born Lewis Freeman on February 28, 1891, in Glasgow, Scotland. He was the seventh child of Julius and Esther Freeman; all of the older children—Philip, Samuel, Maurice, Leah, Sarah, and Lazarus—were born in England.[2] Both Lewis Freeman's birth certificate and the 1891 census for Scotland list the Freeman family as living at 24 Ropework Lane and identify Julius as a fur-skin dresser. The city official certifying the birth certificate indicated that Julius had signed with an *X*. It is probable that Esther too was illiterate, and this may explain why the newborn *Lewis* eventually became *Louis*.

Julius and Esther were married in Riga, Latvia, on May 13, 1878.[3] According to Scottie's nephew Alan Freeman, they landed at Hull, England, around 1880 and were given the name Freeman by the immigration officer.[4] Hull was a common port of entry, especially for those arriving from Eastern Europe. In the last two decades of the nineteenth century there was a great increase in the number of Jews arriving in England, either to make new homes there or to travel on to America.[5]

It is not certain where the Freeman family lived in England, as they do not appear in the 1881 census. But it is most likely they lived in Spitalfields, Whitechapel, London, where there was a large Jewish population. Sometime between the birth of Lazarus in 1889 and that of Lewis in 1891, the Freemans moved to Glasgow. The family of nine settled into a home in the Gorbals section of the city, on the south side of the River Clyde. Much later Scottie joked that it was "the wrong side of the river."

Glasgow's Jewish community was growing rapidly in the final decades of the nineteenth century because of the influx of immigrants from the Continent as well the migration of Jews from England seeking work.[6] Jewish culture permeated this area, and Yiddish was widely spoken. Jewish day schools were established, and merchants used signs with Hebrew lettering. Despite the accessibility of education, Jewish and otherwise, Scottie left school at the age of nine. He never spoke of the reasons for it but later was proud of the fact that he was never hemmed in by the educational system.

Scottie was also quite proud of the jobs he held at such a young age. He sold newspapers, helped vendors set up market stalls, and did some street trading, including selling herbal medicine with one of his older brothers.[7] Scottie reminisced about this medicinal concoction, which "tasted like port wine and was very good for varicose veins." And, he reported, his brother still drank the stuff.[8] In later years he would refer to another early job as a "barefoot" newsboy. Perhaps it was because of this experience that he developed a habit of carrying a newspaper, which he thought would hide the fact that he could barely read.

While the story of the street-urchin newsboy and his family certainly presents a vivid picture, it is unclear how accurate it is. Scottie had a knack for exaggerating and obfuscating the truth; sometimes it seems that he went along with whatever tale was spun by individuals interested in his life. As for his accounts of youthfully running amok in the streets of Glasgow, he later told a journalist that this was "all nonsense, of course. Every boy went barefoot in those days. I had enough money to go to music halls and real music halls they were then. And I can remember a shining clear fountain."[9] Mamie Crichton described his childhood environment: "A large family in a tenement room-and-kitchen meant that much of his early boyhood was spent in the streets, pinching apples from stalls, running errands for ha'pences, venturing as far as Glasgow Green and the banks of the Clyde, a roving explorer in a world where the rewards went to the quick of wit and the fleet of foot."[10]

By the turn of the century, the remaining three children had been born, and the Freeman family must have been in financial difficulty. This is the point at which the family unit can no longer be traced. The family does not appear in the 1901 census for Scotland or England, and a search for the children's names, with appropriate ages, produced no results. The family appears to have vanished.

It is interesting to note that no record was found of Scottie Wilson ever talking about what happened to his family during that period. One can speculate that one or both parents had died or that the father was no longer able to support the family and that the younger children had been placed with other families or in an orphanage. By the time of the 1901 census, the family would have included Philip, twenty-two; Samuel, nineteen; Maurice, seventeen; Leah, sixteen; Sarah, fourteen; Lazarus, twelve; and Louis (Scottie), ten, along with the three younger children: David, Charlie, and Bess. Some of the older children were no doubt living elsewhere.

In spite of coming from a large family, Scottie maintained a highly independent, and rather solitary, lifestyle. Those early years peddling newspapers and shilling patent medicines for his brother taught him some basic skills that would serve him well throughout his life. He always managed to make a living. He was a street-savvy hustler and a survivor.

Red Fish Blue Fish in Brown Circle, 1960–72 (detail of plate 25)

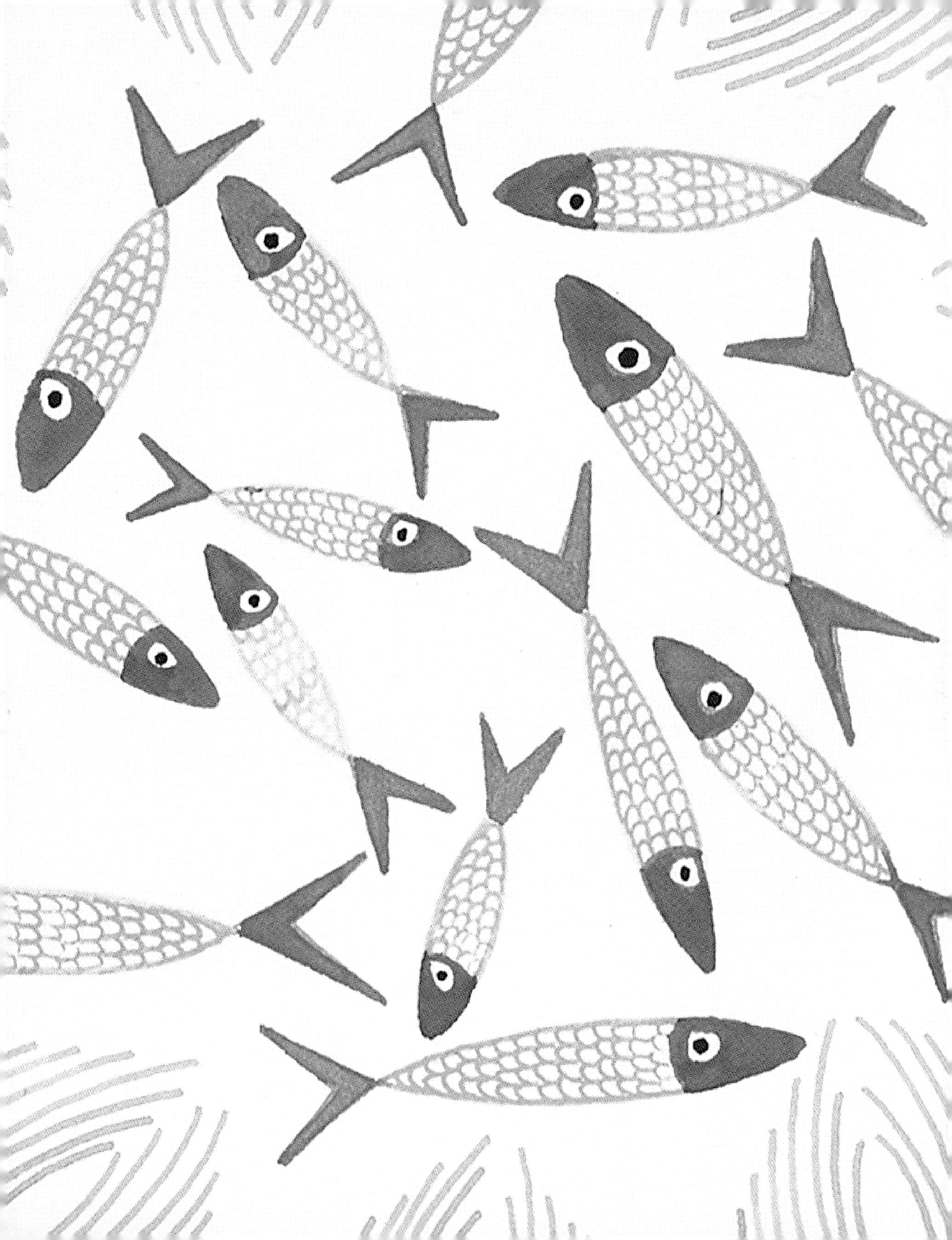

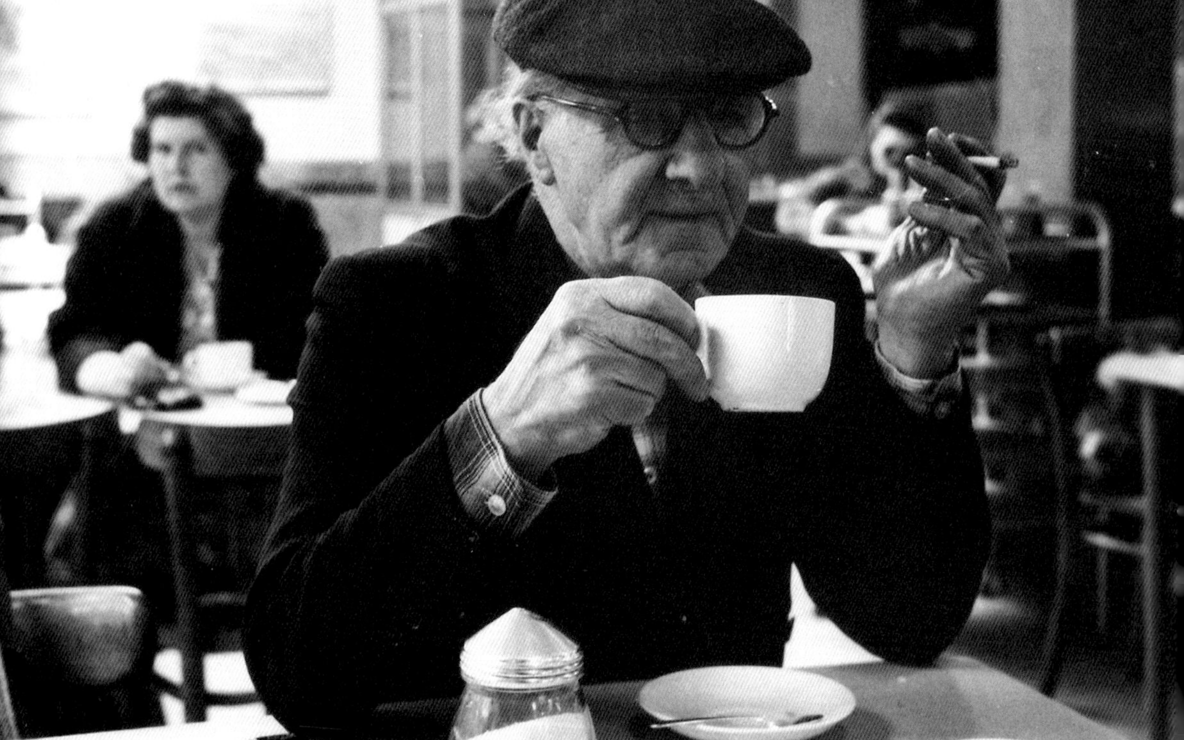

Military Service, 1906–c. 1920

In 1906, at age fifteen, Scottie joined the first battalion of the Cameronians,[11] also known as the Scottish Rifles. Founded in 1689, the regiment—named in honor of Richard Cameron, a Covenanter and defender of the Presbyterian faith—was based on the principle of the "Bible and the Sword." Upon enlisting, Scottie was sent to India, where the first battalion had been deployed since 1894. During his three years there, the battalion was camped at Meerut and Chakrata. In 1909 the Cameronians left Bombay for South Africa, disembarked at Durban, and traveled to Tempe, about four miles from Bloemfontein. There they took over duties from the second battalion of the Argyll and Sutherland Highlanders.

By March 1912 it was assumed that war with Germany was inevitable. In preparation for the conflict, the Cameronians were relieved and sent back to Maryhill Barracks in Glasgow, having served for eighteen years in India and South Africa. Some months prior, however, Scottie, now age twenty, bought himself out of the army after five years of service. He liked to boast that he had won a large sum of money in a Crown and Anchor dice game, which financed his return to civilian life. It was enough to buy his way out but not enough for the passage home. So the ever-enterprising young man worked his way back to Glasgow as a ship's stoker.

Once back in Scotland, Scottie sometimes stayed with his sister Sarah's family in Kilmarnock, about twenty miles south of Glasgow.[12] At the outbreak of World War I Scottie rejoined the Cameronians to serve on the Western Front.[13] On August 13, 1914, the battalion embarked on the S.S. *Caledonia* at Southampton for Le Havre. In France the Cameronians immediately took up positions as part of the nineteenth brigade, whereupon they met heavy resistance from German troops.

Little is known about Scottie's military experiences.[14] He did not speak much about these years, and subsequent interviews yield scant information. A few rare

Scottie Wilson, c. 1965–70. Photographer: Ida Kar (1908–74). National Portrait Gallery, London.

comments about his service in France during World War I are recorded. He told one journalist: "I was always going in for anything to get out of duties. The sergeant-major would come up to me and say 'Scottie, you're a funny little blighter, what're you doing?' and I'd say I was training for the football team, or wrestling. Later I got tired of the Army and told the Colonel I was fed up and wanted to get away from the Front."[15] Another rare anecdote about this period was told by Dr. Clifford Myerson to author George Melly, who wrote:

> *Scottie was in France and advancing with his platoon through a wood where there was a fork and the order was to take the left-hand path. Those ahead of him who did so were mowed down so Scottie quite deliberately turned to the right and eventually found himself at a Red Cross Unit where, for three days, he helped carry in the wounded. Once when he was sleeping, a Colonel arrived, saw him and asked who he was and what he was doing there. It might have gone badly for him if it hadn't been for the surgeon in charge who praised his courage under fire, and no further enquiries were made.*[16]

There are varying accounts of what Scottie was doing from the end of his service in World War I until the early 1930s. According to his friend Mervyn Levy, "After the war he went back to street trading; in Glasgow and then in London. He sold anything he could from cigars to junk. In London he took a stall in the old Caledonian Market and later a shop in the Edgware Road. He then went to Canada, returned to England, and in the early thirties he felt compelled to return to Canada."[17]

Only a few people knew the real story of Scottie's post–World War I activities. He did not generally reveal that a year or two after the war had ended he had joined the Black and Tans,[18] a group of former British soldiers recruited and sent to Ireland to assist the Royal Irish Constabulary (RIC) with suppressing the Irish Republican Army (IRA). To help recruit veterans, the British government had opened recruitment offices in various cities, including Glasgow.

Scottie and other war veterans had returned from the Western Front to find a depressed economy. They didn't join the Black and Tans because they believed in the mission; they joined because it was a job, for which they were paid ten shillings a day (the equivalent of about thirteen pounds sterling or twenty dollars today).[19] The term of duty was indefinite. Like most soldiers, past and present, they were ill prepared to be good policemen. The selection standards were greatly relaxed to aid in attracting recruits, and the men were poorly trained and supervised. The Black and Tans were so hastily assembled that they didn't even have complete uniforms. They wore a mixture of military khaki and the dark RIC police uniforms, resulting in the nickname Black and Tans. Their assignment was to make the country "a hell for rebels to live in." And hell they made it—for the IRA, for themselves, and mostly for the civilians.

The Black and Tans eventually numbered about ten thousand. These ex-servicemen found it difficult to cope with the guerrilla tactics of the IRA and were brutal in their retaliation against attacks on their own ranks. One of bloodiest exchanges occurred in November 1920. Twelve civilians died when the Black and Tans opened fire on a crowd of spectators in Dublin's Croake Park, following the IRA killing of fourteen of their men. The IRA in turn massacred eighteen members of the "Auxies" (an auxiliary force to the Black and Tans), which incited the auxiliaries to set fire to the center of the city of Cork.

In the two and a half years that the RIC and Black and Tans spent fighting the IRA, more than 1,300 people died (550 of them troops and police). Yet there was still no peace. Irish and British public opinion turned against the British government, and the Black and Tans were disbanded at the end of 1921. The secretary of state for war and air during that time was Winston Churchill. John Keegan has written:

> *Churchill . . . argued for fighting things out, and supported the creation of military anti-terror units—the Black and Tan, the "Auxies"—that adopted the terrorist methods of the Irish Republican Army (IRA). Eventually convinced that the IRA could not be overcome, so strong was its support among the Catholic population, he agreed to accept first the partition of Ireland into a large Catholic South and small Protestant North, then to direct negotiations with the leaders of the IRA to bring about a settlement. . . . Ireland was the worst of the problems to confront Churchill in his postwar appointments as secretary of state for war and then for the colonies.*[20]

But before it was disbanded, Scottie Wilson quit the Black and Tans, presumably without permission. Perhaps he no longer wanted to be a party to the killings and the atrocities. Clifford Myerson, who was his doctor for the last five years of his life, said that Scottie had "deserted the army." Scottie then hid out in a house in Ireland with several IRA men who had impressed him deeply. And Scottie's nephew Alan Freeman likewise reported that his uncle absconded, leaving Ireland for Canada.[21] Even Scottie later made reference to his "first" trip to Canada. But he never said why he went to Canada the first time, how long he stayed, or what he did while there.

Given Scottie's years of military experience, there is little doubt that he thought that he had done something wrong, be it desertion or otherwise, by quitting the Black and Tans. Even though the Black and Tan enlistment was "indefinite," there must have been a formal discharge procedure. But considering the awful publicity the British government received from the entire operation against the IRA, it may later have overlooked many "quits."

Not much is known of Scottie's first stay in Canada, except that he was probably dealing in secondhand goods or picking up odd jobs.[22] His time in Canada is thought to have been quite brief—as short as a few months—before he returned to London and his street-trading activities at the old Caledonian Market.[23] His homecoming may have been prompted by information that he would not be prosecuted for deserting the Black and Tans. The British government could hardly have punished deserters for refusing to be thugs, thieves, and killers of civilians. It no doubt wished that everyone would forget the whole episode. But even today the mere mention of the Black and Tans conjures up associations with police atrocities.

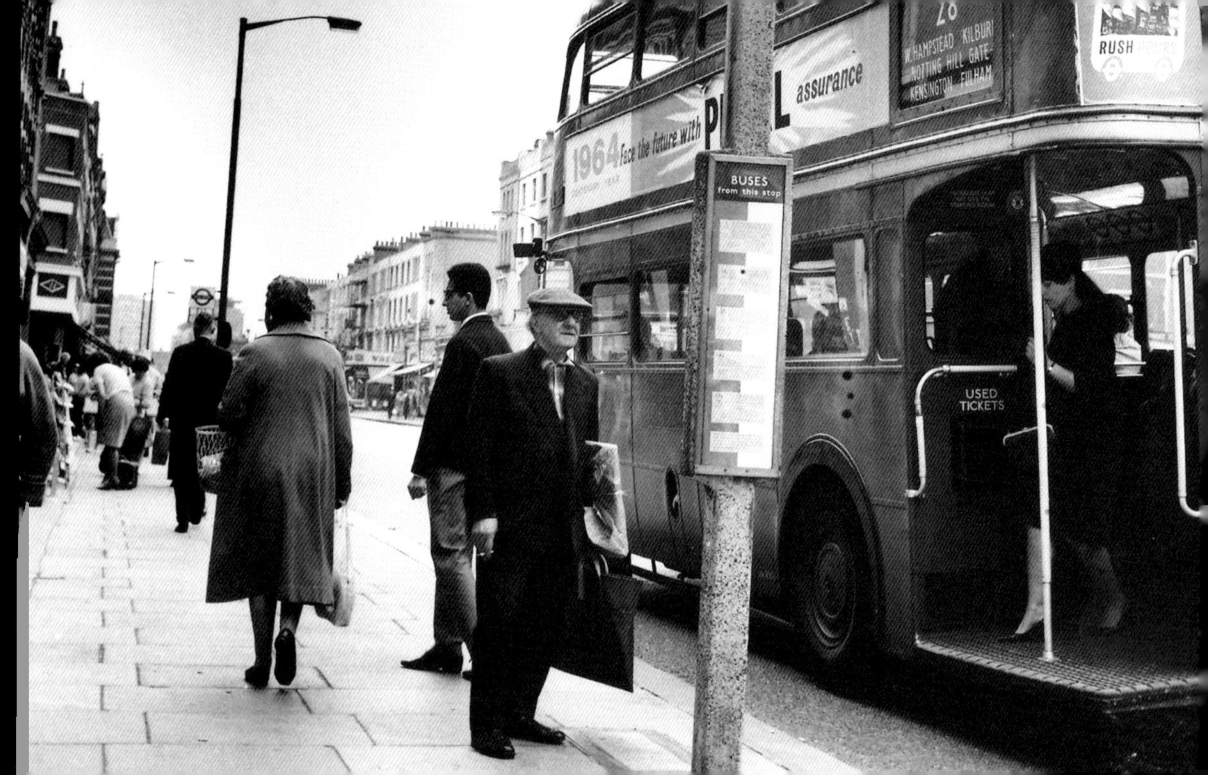
28
W. HAMPSTEAD KILBURN
NOTTING HILL GATE
KENSINGTON FULHAM
RUSH
1964 face the future with P L assurance
BUSES
from this stop
USED
TICKETS

A London Shopkeeper, c. 1922–32

After about a decade and a half of military service in various forms, Scottie settled down for a period in London. To sustain himself, he returned to the secondhand retail trade. This was not an uncommon occupation in the Jewish community at the time, and it would continue to be his chief occupation for the foreseeable future: peddling wares out of a market stand, sometimes even having his own store.[24]

Scottie's businesses most likely included the stall on Caledonian Road, another in Leather Lane, and, most notably, a shop in Edgware Road. The period from 1922 to 1932 would be his longest continuous period of peddling and shopkeeping. Edgware Road is a long commercial street beginning at Marble Arch and heading northwest to the area where Scottie later lived for about twenty years. About a mile up Edgware Road is Church Street, where there has been a collection of stalls for decades, and this may have been where Scottie had his.

Scottie would have found himself in a familiar community, as Jewish families have lived just north of this area for many years. This period is also most likely the time when Scottie lived for a while in King's Cross with an unidentified woman. This was one of many personal disclosures that he made to his confidant Dr. Myerson and one of the few allusions to any relationships he may have had. He readily admitted to the doctor that he had not had much success with women.

The years just prior to 1932 must have been very difficult for Scottie, given the collapse of the British economy. Perhaps he thought that life would be better in Canada. As a British citizen, he could easily travel between Commonwealth nations, so sometime between 1930 and 1932 he set sail for Canada.[25] There is, in fact, an immigration record for one Louis Freeman aboard the *Empress of Britain*, a ship owned by the Canadian Pacific railroad conglomerate, which arrived in Quebec on June 29, 1932.[26]

Scottie Wilson, c. 1965–70. Photographer: Ida Kar (1908–74). National Portrait Gallery, London.

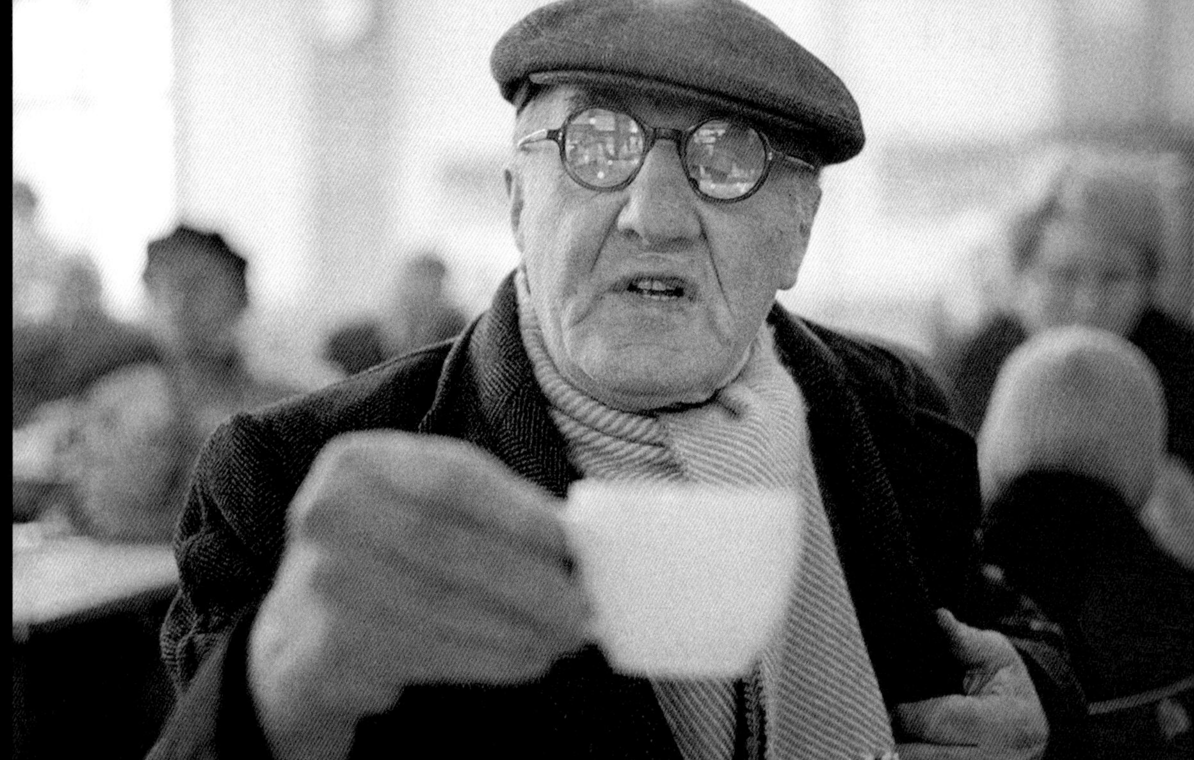

From Peddler to Painter: Canada, 1932–45

Once in Canada, Scottie eventually settled in Toronto. In 1934 he was living in a small bungalow southwest of downtown, still using the name Louis Freeman.[27] He was one of a succession of presumably Jewish boarders who lived at this address over the course of several years. Samuel Richman, a cobbler, used this building as his place of business. There is scant information about Scottie's personal life or activities during this time, but it is significant that he seemed to have been part of the Jewish community in Toronto, as he was in London. He lived at this address until 1937, when he appears to have left the Toronto area.[28]

Scottie continued to earn a living as a peddler and trader. According to him, "You could rent a wee shop in a back street for half-a-crown a week. When I could gather enough stuff that's what I did."[29] His stock-in-trade included cut-glass perfume bottles and fountain pens, which would be stripped of their gold nibs to be sold to a refiner. There are numerous accounts of a secondhand store he had on Yonge Street, although the precise location is a mystery. One account described it as a "little shop on the second floor of a building on Yonge St., just south of Bloor,"[30] and it was there in 1935 that he found his artistic calling.

Scottie told his story to Mervyn Levy:

> [I found a pen that] . . . looked like a bulldog, with a nib as thick as my finger! 14ct gold it was and so unusual, so striking that I said I'm going to keep this pen. I didn't want to break up the bulldog pen with its nib so thick and beautiful. So I kept it.
>
> I took my shop in Yonge Street. A general store it was, and a few days after opening the shop I bought a large table with a thick cardboard top on which to stand my radio. I'm listening to classical music one day—Mendelssohn—when all of a sudden I dipped the bulldog pen into a bottle of ink and started drawing—doodling I suppose you'd call it—on the cardboard tabletop. I don't know why. I just did. In a couple of days—I worked almost ceaselessly—the whole of the tabletop was covered with little faces and designs. The pen seemed to make me draw, and them images, the faces

and designs just flowed out. I couldn't stop—I've never stopped since that day.

Anyway, when the tabletop was full up I bought writing-pads, drawing books, and cheap crayons in Woolworth's and began to develop my own style of working—the pen stroke and the crayon coloring. The drawings poured out, and I began hanging them up all over the shop, and displaying them in the window. I couldn't stop, you see. It just went on and on. And I hadn't any time to look after the shop or the business either, and a friend of mine, a watchmaker named Billy moved in to look after the business for me. I retired behind a curtain where I drew all day.

Then the dealers and critics began calling. Douglas Duncan was the first to take any real interest in my work, and bought it from me in those early days. That's how it all came about. There's nothing you can do; it's a plan; it's all mapped out for you; you just make the moves you must. The bulldog pen was part of the plan, that's all.[31]

Scottie told this story many times to many writers, who were fairly consistent in the retelling, with some elaboration. One writer noted that his inspirational catalyst, the bulldog pen, was bought with a number of other pens from a chemist sometime in late autumn or early winter. Others reveal that the music Scottie was listening to was a radio program of Mendelssohn sponsored by a brewery. Despite all of these supplementary details, it's not certain what the table itself (or its decorated top) actually looked like. There are no known photographs, and its subsequent whereabouts are a mystery. But was it true that the dealers pursued Scottie shortly after he started to draw? That was in fact a gross exaggeration on his part. In reality, Scottie did not enjoy any significant artistic recognition until several years later. It wouldn't be until he had made hundreds of drawings and traveled thousands of miles to several cities before the public would know about this unusual man and his unique art.

Once the tabletop drawing was complete, Scottie, consumed by his new passion, spent hours in the back of his shop, neglecting his business to the point where a friend stepped in and took over for him. His doodles of bizarre faces, flora, and fauna were images that would stay with him for the

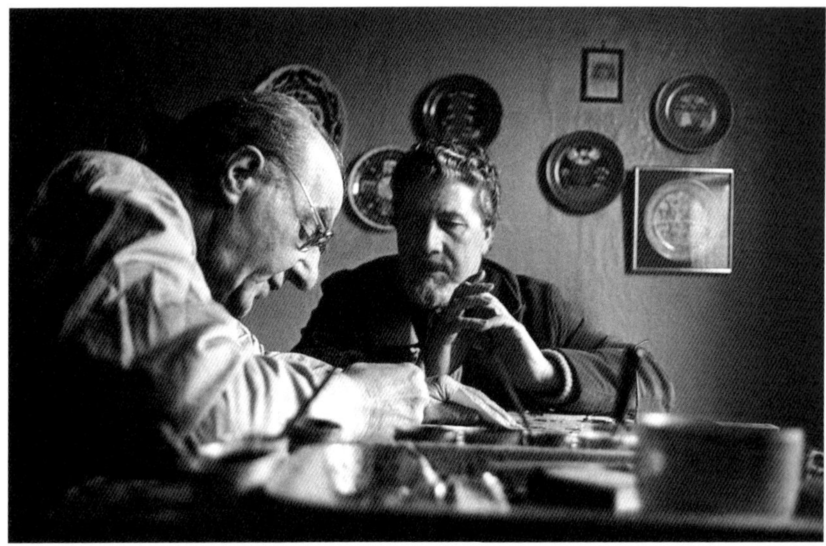

Scottie Wilson at work, with friend Mervyn Levy, at 37 Lynton Road, c. 1965–70.
Photographer: Crispin Eurich (1936–76). © 'The First' Gallery, Southampton, SO18 5DG, www.CrispinEurich.com.

rest of his life. When later asked what his pictures were about, he replied that he was simply "putting his dreams onto paper" and refused to elaborate on whether there was any hidden meaning in his work. To Scottie, if you couldn't understand by looking at it, there was just no use in trying to explain. "Aye, birds, trees, and flowers—that's me. Don't ask me what they mean. If you don't know I can't tell you. Some people can feel it; were born with it."[32]

Scottie was more willing to talk about the way he created than about what his pictures meant. He explained: "I paint when the mood comes on me. The ideas come to me in dreams: sometimes I get an original idea from something I see in the bus, say, a chimney in the distance, then in my mind's eye I do the rest by elaborating on the chimney with fields, people, houses, and so on."[33] Scottie's dreams and imaginings provided inspiration for his work, but he molded them into sophisticated compositions.

The impulses for Scottie's art were swift and sudden, but they didn't always come easily. Journalist Paul Duval wrote: "Scottie would have to wait for a dream . . . before he could create. During periods of inactivity, he complained that he was 'all dreamt out.'"[34] Scottie commented to another reporter that he needed to be happy to work, and to be alone. He couldn't create when he felt intruded upon. Additionally, "Mr. Wilson once confessed that when he sits down in front of a blank sheet of paper he has no idea what will happen. His only fear is that one day nothing will."[35]

Interviewed by a Vancouver newspaper in June 1943, when he was still in the nascent phase of his long artistic career, Scottie related: "I've come a long way since my early doodling years ago. . . . I've gradually gained more and more feeling for design and now each picture has to be just right before I can call it finished."[36] He knew when it was right, when it was finished, but didn't know how he did it.

The leitmotifs of his work did not change over four decades, but this is not to say that his style did not change. Certain images became more prevalent, while others were used less frequently. Despite seemingly obvious evidence of development in his oeuvre and the existence of a few records and documents that can place certain works in a specific period, any chronological organization of his output is ultimately speculative, as Scottie signed his works but did not date them. The discussion of the development of his work presented here is based largely on stylistic analysis.

The earliest pieces seem to be those with a more organic composition and looser hatch marks. The forms are less solid, and the impression is one of embryonic and spontaneous creation. Marine creatures, tortoise-like figures, and the ubiquitous fish make early appearances, like prehistoric forerunners of the elegant and sophisticated flora and fauna that would decorate his later drawings. The eyes of his creatures are bulbous and exaggerated, wide-eyed and wondering, not yet the perilous visions of the following years.

The images can be read as amalgamations of Scottie's childhood and recollections of family life as well as his travels. As a young boy he enjoyed the zoo and was very fond of animals. Birds play a significant role in his work, especially in the middle and late years, as do fish. His drawings became havens for plumed swans and Vancouver diving ducks.[37] Characters that Scottie included in his art may find their roots in his personal experiences, and it has been noted by many that the recurring face with droopy eyes and large, bulbous nose looks distinctly like a self-portrait. Comparisons between these images and photos of Scottie Wilson do nothing to refute this idea.

Other figures, especially two mustached faces, are said to be images of the artist's brothers (but which brothers from his large family is difficult to say). One cryptic account describes the appearance of these siblings in his work: "He always sets them on candle holders. Three of them have a calm look and the fourth, named Frank, always looking at the sky, because it is Scottie who said it, he's the only good one, all the others are scoundrels."[38]

Some have speculated about the existence of veiled sexual references in Scottie's work, as in Victor Musgrave's assessment that "the masculine element is as often repeated in fishes, vases, cupolas, spires, cones, chimneys and crosses as the female one is in circles, orifices, fish-ponds, petals and ovals of all kinds."[39] Given the organic nature of Scottie's imagery, however, it seems only logical that his drawings contain elongated and rounded forms, the selection of which does not seem to suggest a hidden iconography, but rather grows out of the working process and intended visual outcome.

On the question of source material for Scottie's work, it is not implausible that some of these intricate and exotic images could have been souvenirs of his military sojourns in India and South Africa. Characteristically, Scottie denied this when writer Mamie Crichton asked about the possibility of these influences, specifically in reference to his later tableware designs. She recorded the exchange: "My high-falutin' suggestion got the answer it deserved. The mischievous old face filled with a curious innocence and wonder as he said: 'There were swans on the Clyde, and flowers and trees in Glasgow Green. I was drawing them. And do you mind the fountain? That was beautiful.'"[40]

Scottie had no obvious interest in conventionally representational pictures, but recorded his dream visions and responses to the world around him. A reviewer of his work gave an example: "he one day saw a man that to him symbolized everything that is greedy and covetous. What he thought of that man has been put down on paper in the form of a picture and it is a blind man who cannot see what the artist has intended him to see."[41] Scottie's early works sometimes included frightening visages with menacing eyes and teeth, which were termed "evils" and "greedies," but his later works are utopian windows into a peaceful, serene landscape of tranquil castles, swans, and flowers. Victor Musgrave aptly described the arc of his oeuvre, reflecting that, "he was constructing a cosmos in which a battle is fought between innocents and evil, beauty and ugliness, and in which goodness ultimately survives."[42]

Comparisons of Scottie Wilson's images show that he was interested throughout his career in working in series, using the same framing technique or compositional elements—circular modules, lozenges, boxy frames, or diagonal corners—in numerous pieces. These similarities in arrangement as well as theme and style suggest pieces that date to common periods, although this cannot be ascertained through any means other than stylistic evidence.

Regardless of the subject, it was rendered in Scottie's own unmistakable and articulate way. He began by drawing the large, dominant shapes in the composition first, then added color and ink to make his signature hatch marks.[43] Forms were outlined and emphasized through his selective coloration and then given texture through his linear technique, using arrays of parallel lines to distinguish areas of the picture. The color fluctuates over and under the inked lines, alternating even within the same picture, demonstrating the flexibility of his working methods.

Although he varied his compositional arrangements, Scottie used mostly crayon, pen, and ink until his later years, when his use of gouache prompted deviations from his usual techniques. He did explore other art tools and methods, reportedly including oil paint on canvas, which turned out to be clumsy and unsuitable for his techique. About his experimentation with watercolor, he said, "The water color took too long to dry before I could apply the ink and when I'm in the mood, I like to work fast and furiously until I get my inspiration onto paper."[44] He did not do preliminary sketches but worked directly to capture the spontaneous image. A later acquaintance recounted a story of Scottie sitting down to his lunch in a café but then, struck by a sudden vision, rushing off to his brushes and pens, leaving his food uneaten.[45]

Though Scottie's work was a solitary pursuit, there were other people who had a significant effect on his development and success as an artist. Although the story of the Toronto tabletop is well known, what is not so well understood is the role of a mysterious woman who saw the completed tabletop at Scottie's Yonge Street shop. Victor Musgrave wrote:

> *Now, for the first time since I had known him, [Scottie] mentioned [a woman] in what was more than a passing aside—on the wife of a friend or a collector. This was a woman whom he said he respected, admired and loved, a clever and perceptive businesswoman.*
>
> *I could not bring myself to enquire into the relationship, but for some reason I felt it was platonic. When she saw the completed card table she told Scottie he was a born artist. It sounded so silly to him he thought she had gone crazy. It appeared that this woman, for reasons of her own, then withdrew from whatever involvement she had in his life, saying that he had something to give the world. . . . When he spoke of her years later, his voice had a catch in it. He could not forget her.[46]*

Scottie told Musgrave in a taped interview in 1964 that he had declined the offer of a "shrewd woman" to go with her to her parents' farm in Quebec, then was heartbroken when she told him that she was terminating their relationship—whereupon he took off to Vancouver to forget her.[47] Was she the same woman who called him a "born artist," or was it another woman? Was he so distraught that he had to move all the way across the Rockies?

On the subject of relationships, E. L. T. Mesens reported in a 1946 *Horizon* article that Scottie "would like to settle down . . . with a nice well-mannered lady who would play the piano, the violin, the harp, or *even* the organ."[48] Whether or not Scottie was serious is open to question. He did like to give writers a good line to print. In today's media world he would be considered a master of the sound bite.

This mysterious woman was apparently not the only one who provided early encouragement for Scottie's art. According to an April 1956 article in the *Edmonton Museum of Art Bulletin*:

> *The first artist to make friends with [Scottie] was Rudy Renzius, the wood-carver and designer in pewter. In 1935 Scottie showed him some small but highly imaginative drawings of fantastic, many-eyed creatures. . . . He had made a few drawings but it is doubtful if he had done any serious work in colour before Renzius met him. But, when Renzius urged him to concentrate on painting, he took this advice so seriously that in the winter of 1942 he closed his business and decided to go into seclusion to devote full time to his art. . . . Scottie went to Winnipeg in below zero weather. There he hired a steam-heated room and painted for months.*[49]

Scottie may or may not have been in Winnipeg in 1942; prior to this time, he traveled across the continent to Vancouver. In a letter to the editor written in response to a newspaper article on a Scottie Wilson exhibition in 1982, Ronald Hambleton, who knew Scottie personally, states that he was in Vancouver much earlier. Hambleton wrote that he met Scottie in Vancouver around 1938, and Scottie "was occupying (I would not say living in) a vacant store on Georgia St."[50] Hambleton was under the impression that Scottie had arrived there from Australia (which is erroneous), but he was carrying on his trading activities, being in possession of a number of boxes of opals. Hambleton recalled, "There were certainly opals there, boxes of them, and one of his activities was to imbed them like tesserae in plaster to make a kind of abstract design." Nothing further is indicated about Scottie's mosaic-like creations or the opals—how they were obtained or what he did with them—but the question of how the seemingly poverty-stricken artist obtained a quantity of semiprecious stones is certainly an interesting one. Hambleton's firsthand account appears to be reliable, but it does little to dispel the aura of mystery surrounding Scottie Wilson.

It should not be forgotten that sometime and somewhere in Canada, Louis Freeman became Scottie Wilson. When Scottie arrived in Canada, he was still identified by his given name, Louis Freeman, and it seems that he continued to be Louis Freeman during his time in Toronto in the 1930s. With his departure for Vancouver, probably sometime in 1936 or 1937, he may have taken up the name under which he would become known as an artist: Scottie Wilson. A few early pictures show a neat cursive signature, "L. Freeman," which has been rubbed out, and in its place is Scottie's early signature: a large, swooping capital *S* nestling the rest of his name inside of one of its curves. Curator Helen Marzolf believes that the cursive handwriting of the "L. Freeman"

signature is not Scottie's.[51] The fact that very few early pictures have this unique
feature seems to indicate that he did not begin to sign his pictures until well after
he had begun drawing.

Scottie never gave a reason for his name change. Possible reasons include the
desire to have a name more reflective of his heavy Glaswegian accent, the wish to avoid
a possible link to his desertion from the Black and Tans, and the desire to blend
in with Canadian society and avoid being a target of anti-Semitism. Careful consideration
of his character, the times, and his immigrant status, however, strongly suggests that
Louis Freeman changed his name to Robert "Scottie" Wilson in response to the growing
anti-Semitism in Canada. Scottie knew that a typically Scottish name would be much
better for business than a Jewish one. And despite his heavy accent, he would be much
less likely to experience the open hostility directed at many immigrants, especially
Jewish immigrants. Changing one's name wasn't that unusual; millions of immigrants
to North America had altered or changed their names during the nineteenth and
twentieth centuries.[52]

Around the time Scottie landed in Quebec in 1932, Canadian hostility to existing
and prospective immigrants had reached a boiling point. With the stress brought on by
the depressed economy during this time of hardship and rampant unemployment—
nearly one-fourth of the Canadian population was without work in 1933—animosity
grew toward waves of immigrants that had previously streamed into the county. Legislation
restricted immigration, making it difficult for Jewish refugees from Nazi Germany
to enter Canada. Those who had already begun to make a new life there were required
to have established themselves through a term of residency of up to five years, depending
on their country of origin, and to maintain gainful employment or risk deportation.
British subjects faced less stringent rules, however, and were required to have domiciled
in Canada for only one year.[53]

Historically the cultural makeup of Toronto was heavily British and Protestant, and
in the early twentieth century the city was permeated by a xenophobic taint. The Jewish
community was the largest non British ethnic group and, as such, subject to prejudice.[54]
Anti-Semites were vocal, and even some Canadian politicians freely expressed anti-Jewish
sentiments. The prejudice was less noticeable in western Canada, where Scottie later
lived. Yet Scottie must have felt some sense of "roots" in Toronto. In 1932 the city had
a Jewish population of 46,751, about 7 percent of its 630,000 residents. Records
indicate that 3,571 Jewish men and 1,671 Jewish women worked in clothing manufacturing—
46 percent of all the workers in that industry.[55] The garment district was in the Spadina
area, only a few blocks from Scottie's shop on historic Yonge Street.

So it was in this environment that Scottie set out to establish himself, and it is
likely that he changed his name in order to blend more easily into Canadian society.
But given his secret Zionist beliefs, there is no doubt that he continued to resent the
treatment of Jews in Canada and that country's unwillingness to allow Jews fleeing the

Nazis into the country. George Melly wrote that Scottie made no attempt to conceal his Jewish identity when he spoke with his doctor and close friend, Clifford Myerson. In fact, he revealed himself as a passionate Zionist. "'He took it for granted, and incorrectly,' says Dr Myerson, 'that I was an equally committed Zionist. I saw no point in correcting him. It would only have upset him.' Dr Myerson confirms Scottie's obsession with anti-Semitism, a word, which like so many others, he pronounced incorrectly."[56]

According to Victor Musgrave, Scottie told him that he suddenly left Toronto after ending an association with an unidentified woman and went to Vancouver, more than four thousand miles away.[57] In this Pacific port city Scottie took up residence in the Chinese quarter,[58] established by immigrants who had come during the Gold Rush years. It is interesting to note that he chose this area, filled with people who maintained their own customs and traditions, distinct from those of the mainstream Vancouver population. He would have been immersed in this culture thanks to the location of his home and his business dealings, but one can only speculate about whether Chinese motifs and imagery had any impact on his artwork.

In Vancouver Scottie continued his drawing and trading activities. As Stuart Underhill has noted: "Painting remained his chief preoccupation but his trading instincts provided the bread and butter, whether he was dealing in used clothing or buying odd lots of jam from canneries and selling it to Chinese restaurants for fruit pie."[59] Thus, all seemed "business as usual" for Scottie in Vancouver.

While living in the Chinese quarter of Vancouver may have shaped Scottie's experiences during this time, there is another key aspect of the city that would have made a deep impression on him, and that is Stanley Park.[60] Not only did the park appeal to Scottie's love of nature, but the it was also home to totem poles from various Northwest Coast Indian cultures, including Nuu-chah-nulth, Kwakiutl, Haida, and Nishga.[61] The curious visages found on these totem poles have long been identified as an influence on the stacked structures and exaggerated faces in his work. When similarities were noted by Mervyn Levy, Scottie said only, "Yes, that's true, but the totem poles are my totem poles."[62]

The year 1942 marked a critical point in Scottie's travels in Canada.[63] Some sources state that this was the year he moved to Vancouver, and others, such as the *Edmonton Museum of Art Bulletin* article cited above, maintain that he moved to Winnipeg. This was also the year that Scottie, having consulted a representative of the Federation of Canadian Artists in Winnipeg, met the organization's national secretary, Rik Kettle, who was also involved with the Picture Loan Society in Toronto. Kettle encouraged Scottie to meet Douglas Duncan, who became his most important Canadian advocate and arguably helped Scottie truly establish himself as an artist.

As disjointed as these events may seem, if one pulls them together, a story emerges that suggests that there may be a grain of truth in each. Scottie recounted that he left

Toronto and went to Vancouver as a result of ending a relationship or association with a French Canadian woman. This is substantiated by Hambleton's recollection of meeting him around 1938,[64] the same year that he entirely disappeared from the Toronto directories. While in Vancouver he continued his trading business as well as drawing. But perhaps in the pivotal year of 1942 Scottie did travel to Winnipeg in the winter months, taking a steam-heated room to work on his drawings. In the interest of furthering his artistic career, he contacted a representative of the Federation of Canadian Artists, an organization newly founded in 1941 to promote Canadian art and artists and establish a useful network of contacts. For reasons unknown, this representative directed him to Toronto, or perhaps he was referred to a contact in that city because he planned on returning there anyway. Thus, at about nine o'clock one evening in 1942, Scottie Wilson arrived unannounced at Rik Kettle's door carrying an enormous bundle of drawings. This was Scottie Wilson the *merchant* at his best.

From this watershed year, Scottie's travels became more frequent, his work was exhibited fairly regularly in a number of Canadian cities, and he began to be recognized for his unique imagery. Perhaps he did indeed decide that the life of an artist was the life for him or that his dedication to his art outweighed any appeal that street trading still had. He still was not keen on parting with his works, but he did put out a plate at his exhibitions for those who wished to donate a few coins. In later interviews, it was revealed that he didn't always have an easy time. One newspaper wrote: "Scottie admits to having been hungry on occasion. At one time he used to take a picture to a restaurant and say, 'You take this. Let me know when I have eaten enough meals to pay for it.'"[65] Scottie later summarized his ideas on the relationship between art and sustenance: "People sometimes say the best art is done by hungry men. I do not believe it."[66]

In 1936, several years before he met Scottie Wilson, Rik Kettle had an idea for a gallery based on an enterprise he learned of in London called the Picture Hire Society. The premise was simple: artists could produce works and show them at the gallery, where they could be bought or merely rented by interested patrons. This opened up the possibility of reaching a new market of art aficionados who perhaps could not afford an outright purchase or who preferred to live with a piece for a while before acquiring it. The artist shared in the revenue from rentals and sales, and the gallery realized additional financial support through membership fees collected from artists and patrons alike.

The Picture Loan Society, as the Canadian version was called, was one of few places where unestablished artists could show their work in 1930s Toronto, but this is not to say that there were no restrictions.[67] Kettle and the others responsible carefully selected artists whom they believed merited the attention. One of the first people Kettle tapped to help establish the gallery was Douglas Duncan, a man known for his discerning eye and devotion to the arts.

When Scottie met with Kettle, he suggested that he see Duncan and arrange for

an exhibition at the Picture Loan Society. This, however, was not exactly what Scottie
had in mind. He did not want to sell his drawings; he merely wanted to charge
admission for people to look at them. It took a great deal of effort on Kettle's part
to coax him into speaking with Duncan and a good deal of gentle persuasion from
Duncan to convince Scottie to actually have a show at the Picture Loan Society. Later,
when describing how he began to show his work in galleries, Scottie would claim that
"the professors" organized it.[68]

The appearance of the singular character of Douglas Duncan was extremely fortuitous
not only for Scottie Wilson but arguably for the whole of the Canadian art world as well.
Duncan was from a wealthy background (his father was the president of Provincial
Paper Limited) and had tried his hand in business but was not cut out for it in aptitude
or temperament. He was an ardent bibliophile, and an extended stay in Paris in his
twenties led him to the craft of bookbinding. He was a great lover of the arts and
spent countless hours visiting galleries, attending the opera and ballet, and reading.
Upon his return to Toronto, he intended to make a living as a binder of fine books.
The market for this distinguished skill was, however, limited. During the years of the
Picture Loan Society, his consuming interest shifted from books to art, and he amassed
a substantial collection of Canadian works, which were eventually bequeathed to the
nation. And for Scottie Wilson, Duncan became his first and perhaps most influential
advocate. Thus, contrary to what Scottie told Mervyn Levy, Duncan became involved
in his artistic career seven years after he began making art, not immediately after he started.

The Picture Loan Society was housed on the third floor of an unassuming old brick
building in the heart of Toronto. The entrance was tucked away on Charles Street
West, just off the bustling thoroughfare of Yonge Street. It was not exactly easy to find,
especially during its later years, due to a complete lack of signage, posted operating
hours, and building directory. But for the intrepid visitor, it was worth the climb up two
long, steep flights of stairs, ending in a narrow hallway that led to four rooms with
light gray walls where pictures were displayed. The gallery exhibitions were usually rotated
for two-week periods, not including summertime, when Duncan would take off for
his lakeside cabin retreat.

The first Scottie Wilson exhibition at the Picture Loan Society took place in late
April 1943.[69] Called *Fantastic Designs by "Scottie"*, the exhibition was reviewed by Pearl
McCarthy for the *Globe and Mail*. McCarthy prophetically wrote about Scottie's works,
"Their importance, in addition to their decorative value, is the possible adaptation of them
to articles of applied art and craft, and the exhibition will establish Scottie's authorship
of them." She also offered an assessment of these unusual works: "In character they
show talent for the grotesque or Gothic mood, but they are modern."[70]

Shortly after the Picture Loan Society show, Scottie uprooted himself again.
Duncan later wrote, rather disparagingly, "A psychopathic restlessness sent him off again,
this time to Vancouver."[71] Back on the Pacific Coast, Scottie did not fare badly;

he had two exhibitions within weeks. The first was a self-promoted show in a borrowed shop at 980 Granville Street, which included between 500 and 750 drawings. He received favorable press coverage for this exhibition of art "by a Glasgow artist, R. Wilson, better known as 'Scottie.'"[72] Scottie himself sat in the window drawing to attract attention. Following his customary practice, he did not offer any of the pictures for sale. He charged no admission (as he would later on), and the only revenue from this venture was in the form of donations from interested visitors.[73]

Scottie's second exhibition of 1943 was at the Vancouver Art Gallery. A representative of this institution saw his storefront display and invited him for a summertime showing. The Vancouver Art Gallery promoted a wide array of work; previous shows of that year included work by Canadian painter Emily Carr and an exhibition entitled *Twenty-five Years of the Soviet Union.* Scottie's work was shown from August 20 to September 9, 1943, concurrently with other short summer exhibitions, including a display of West African masks.

Returning to Toronto, Scottie continued to find outlets for his work. *Colour Drawings by Scottie* opened February 1, 1944, at the Picture Loan Society and was slated to close on February 14 but was held over until March 1. Scottie's work was also included in the *Twenty-first Annual Exhibition of the Society of Graphic Art,* held at the Art Gallery of Toronto. And, being the enterprising sort, he mounted his own exhibition in the nearby town of Saint Catharines, Ontario. As the local newspaper reported: "R. (Scotty) Wilson, Scottish born artist, has set up his exhibit at 299 St. Paul St. and is showing over 500 of his pieces for all who care to come in and view them. Scotty's pictures are not for sale, not at the present time at any rate. . . . From time to time he has sold pictures but he says 'It's like selling my body and soul.' The only reason he has ever sold one is to provide for himself the necessities of life."[74]

In addition to his support in gallery shows, Duncan also kept an inventory and records of approximately 240 of some 600 drawings Scottie did in Canada.[75] If eyewitness accounts are correct and Scottie actually showed 750 drawings in his self-promoted Vancouver exhibition (and this was early in his career), then the number of works he produced in Canada must be considerably higher. Duncan's inventory was arranged in a loosely chronological order and shows Scottie's burgeoning interest in developing thematic motifs in his work. A gradual change from his swooping-*S* signature to the straight-line "Scottie" autograph found on his later works is also evident.

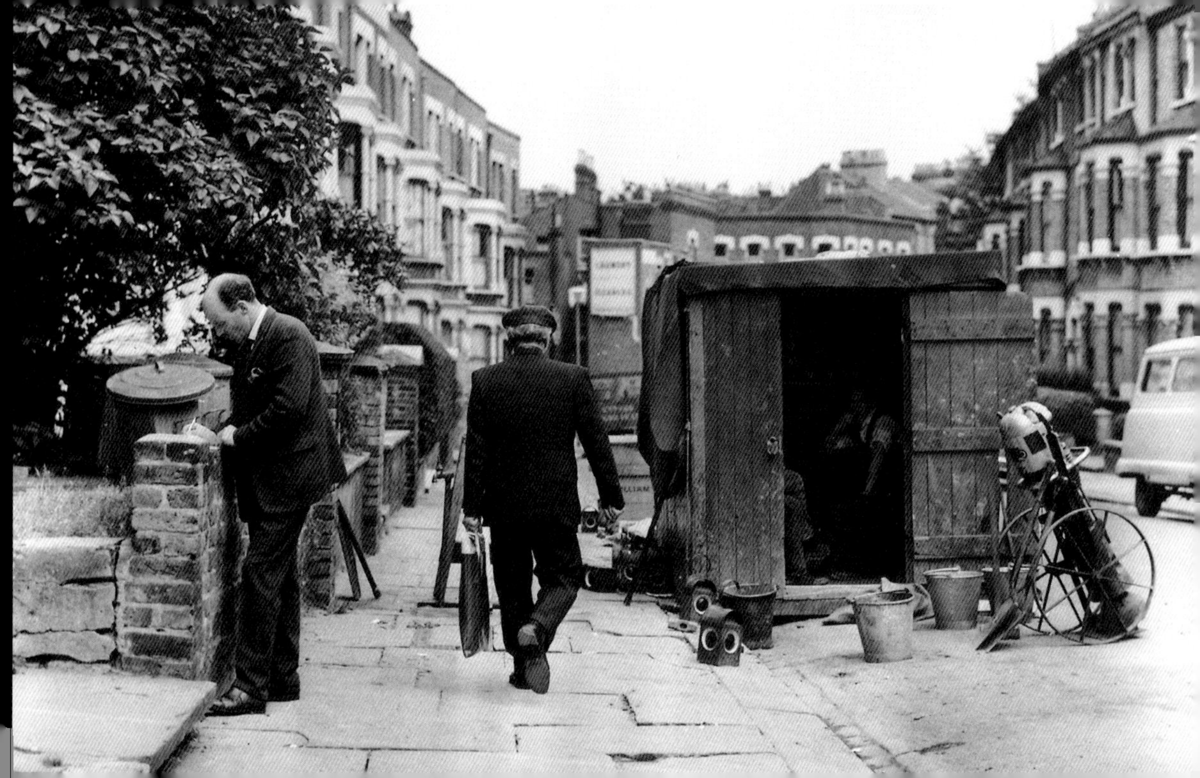

Return to Britain, 1945

The following year, 1945, Scottie again showed his work at the Picture Loan Society
in April, but he was soon to leave Canada for Great Britain. According to correspondence
from Douglas Duncan, he departed in late May or early June. In Duncan's inventory
of Scottie's drawings, there were at least two pieces from that year (and one specifically dated
May 1945) that appear to be unfinished due to their lack of distinctive hatch marks
and incomplete compositions. Presumably these are some of the last pieces Scottie
made in Canada, and he left them in that country with Duncan. Their successful
business relationship came to an abrupt end with Scottie's sudden decision to relocate
once again. He asked Duncan for a loan so that he could return to England, and in
response Duncan wrote the following letter:[76]

> *3 Charles Street West / Toronto*
> *May 23 '45*
>
> *Dear Scottie*
>
> *I had assured you that I would see that you had the necessary money to go if you would wait until
> it was more convenient. It could hardly be less convenient for both of us than it is now; but I guess
> we might as well get it over with, seeing that patience is not one of your virtues.*
>
> *I am enclosing a cheque for $234 (go Friday morning to the bank across from the Picture Loan)
> and $75 in cash. If you can't manage with that, phone me, and maybe I can dig up a little more.
> YOU MUST HAVE $50—PREFERABLY $75—left in your pocket after the boat and rail tickets
> are paid and you leave Toronto.*
>
> *I am sorry I can't straighten things out before you go, check over everything—but I'm sure I won't
> be able to go on Friday, even if I have no fever tomorrow. Everything is mixed up—I brought a number
> of drawings up here with me on Saturday thinking I might photograph them on Sunday. But Sunday
> I was in bed. I'll ask Norman to take a couple of the most recent ones in to you, and the others you
> wanted I will mail to you later. Would you let me buy the one with the silver background? I'm afraid*

*it will get messy no matter how you pack it. And it might be nice to keep just one of the new kind—
one that I like, even if you don't, so much.*

*I had picked out 40 of the very earliest ones that we had in the store-room, and was going
to propose that I buy them. However, such things will have to be done by mail.*

You had better give Norman your broker's address.

*Good-luck to you—I hope the trip will be satisfactory. I will go on with my job of looking after
the ones here and I'll send you the album of photographs when it is a little fuller.*

Yours truly,
Douglas[77]

Clearly Duncan was not happy. Scottie left so quickly that Duncan did not have
time to sort out his inventory or even make him an offer for work he was considering
for purchase. The timing of Scottie's decision is surprising; the war in Europe had
ended only weeks before, but perhaps he had been eagerly awaiting this moment to return
home. As with his other abrupt migrations, Scottie never explained his hasty departure
from Canada to anyone. Perhaps he felt that his opportunities were limited there or just
wanted to show his art to a wider audience. Or his wanderlust may have overcome him
again, and with the war having just ended in Europe, he wasted no time in returning.

When Scottie left London in 1932, he was a mere junk dealer. Since then, much about
his life had changed. His art, which became his consuming interest from the moment
he began drawing on the tabletop in the back of his Toronto shop, was now his chief
occupation. Now he was Scottie Wilson—an accomplished artist with gallery sales, favorable
press reviews, and a newfound passion. For Scottie it was an opportune time to start a new
life. His days of living from hand-to-mouth were ending. No more hawking old perfume
bottles, selling other people's discards, and pocketing a few dollars. Certainly his art career
would be even more successful at home in England and Scotland than it was in Canada.
It had been ten years since he first took pen to paper—a very long apprenticeship—and now
it was time to reap the rewards of a master artist.

Scottie's skills as a self-promoter, honed in Canada, would certainly be of use to him
in England. It was quite a risk he was taking, now that his art provided his income
rather than his old, familiar trade in secondhand goods. He had found a great deal
of support for his drawings in Canada, particularly through Douglas Duncan and
the Picture Loan Society, but was forgoing this network to forge a new one on the other
side of the Atlantic Ocean. Notwithstanding that he was returning to his native soil,
this was foreign territory to Scottie Wilson, the artist.

Although Scottie was returning home, he was a very different person than he was
when he left. Louis Freeman, the shrewd street trader, Jewish son of immigrant parents,
had evolved into the persona of Scottie Wilson: a wily, mysterious Glaswegian Scot. His
physical appearance certainly added to his character; he was a short, slightly stocky man
with mischievous eyes, a bulbous nose, and a nearly impenetrable brogue, a holdover from

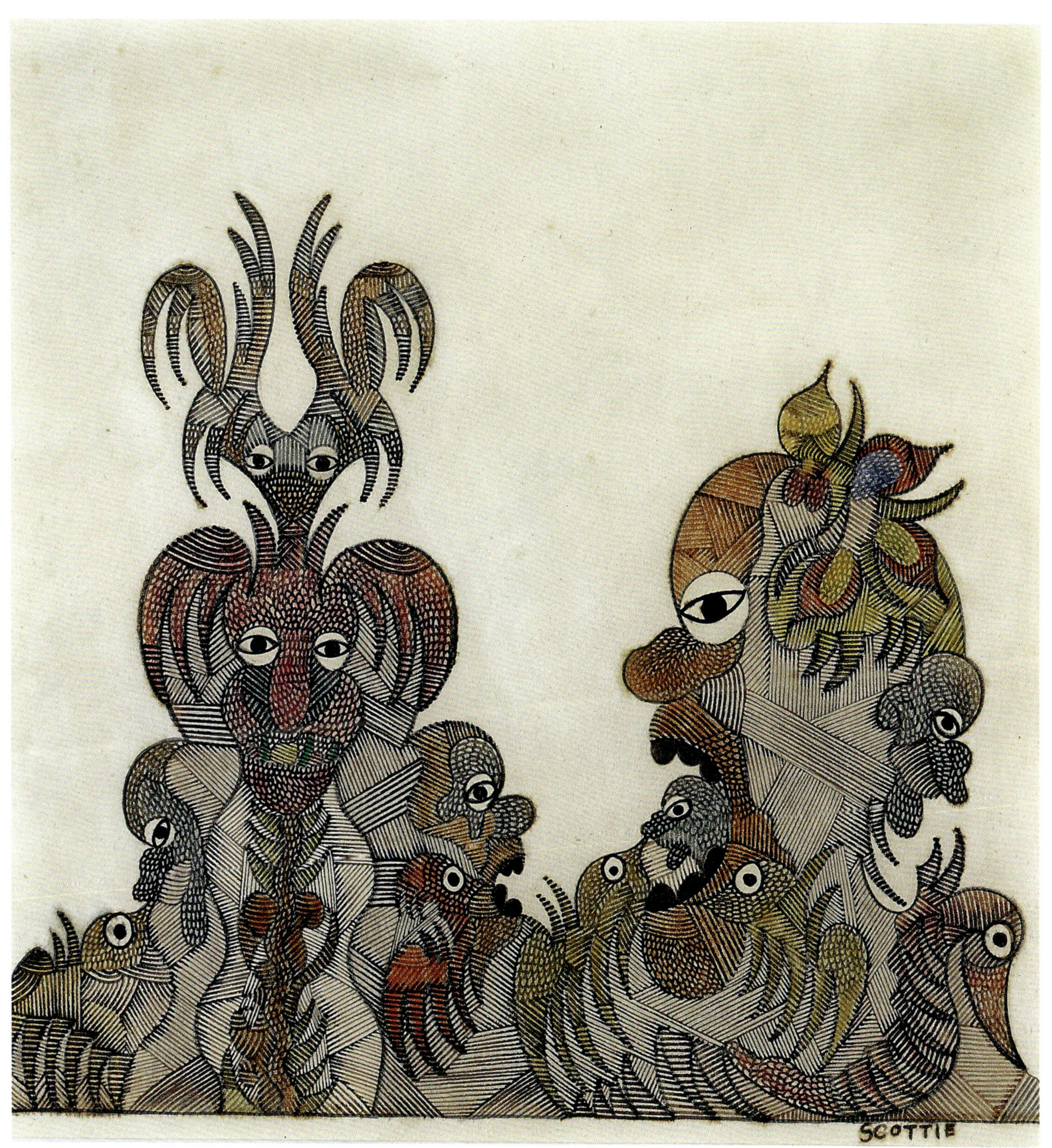

PLATE I. *The Greedies,* c. 1945. Pen, ink, and watercolor on paper. 11 x 11 inches (27.9 x 27.9 centimeters).

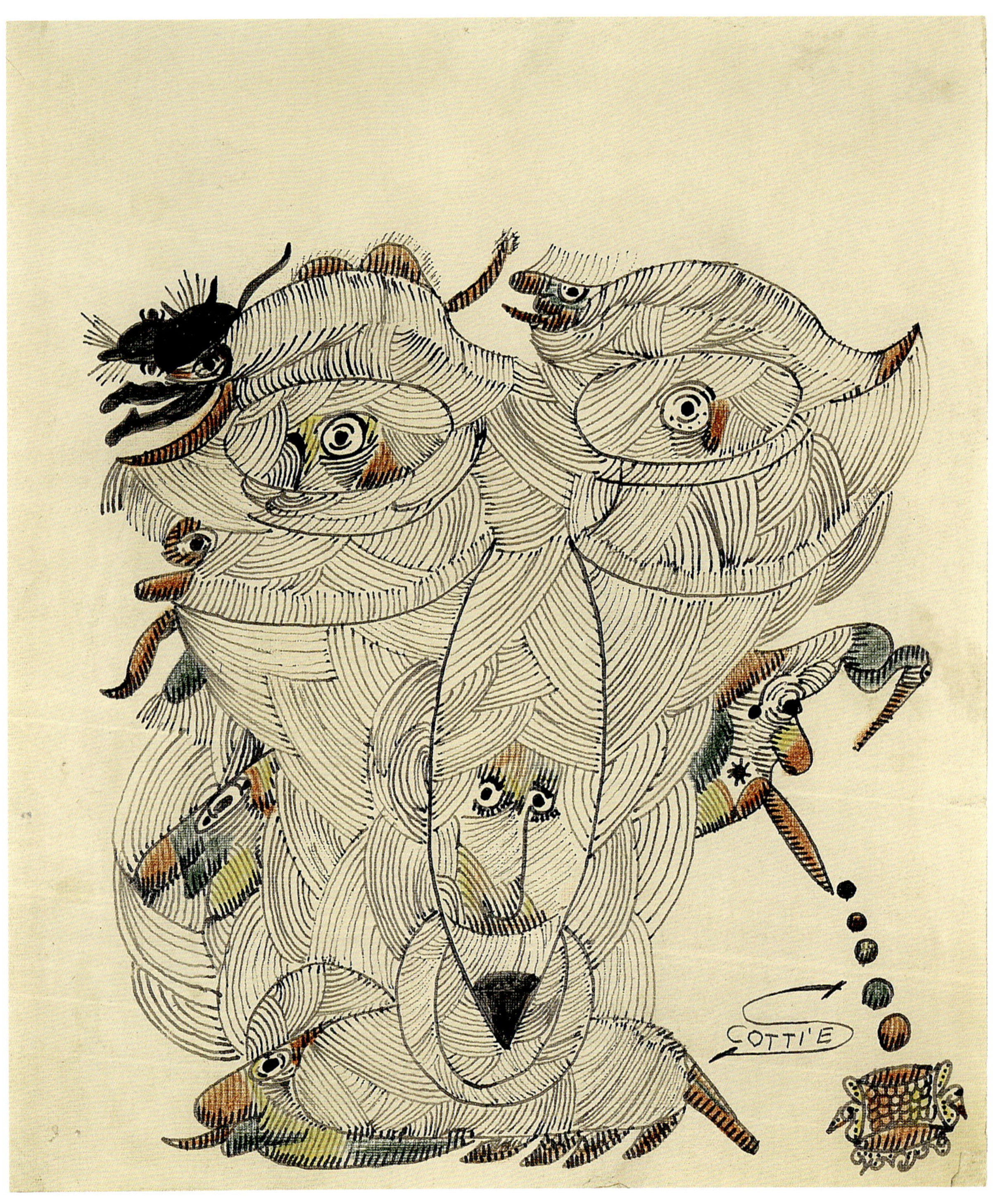

PLATE 2. *Black Mouse*, c. 1935. Pen, ink, and crayon on paper. 9$\frac{1}{2}$ x 8 inches (24.1 x 20.3 centimeters).

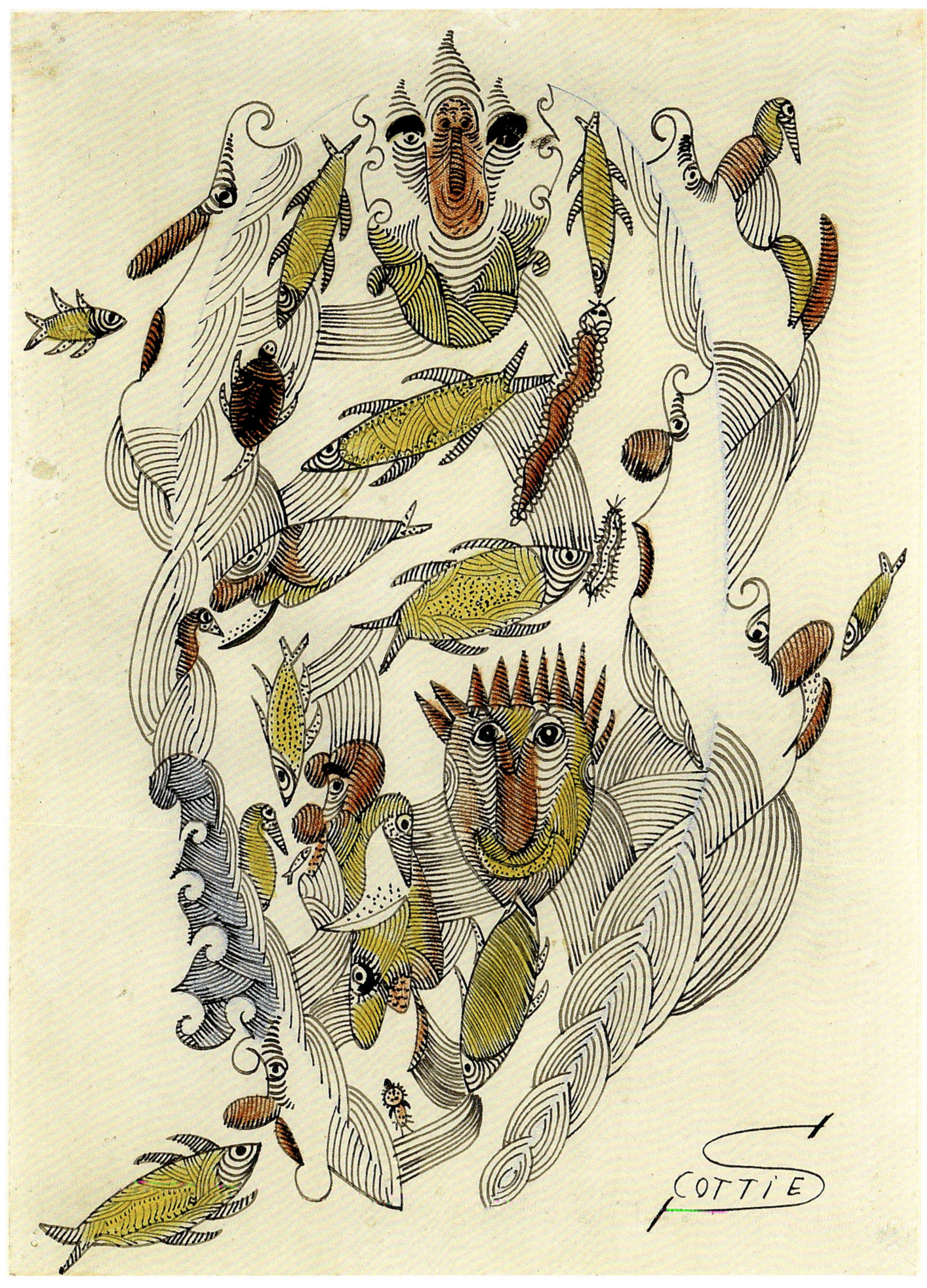

PLATE 3. *Yellow Fish and Faces,* c. 1935. Pen, ink, and crayon on paper. II $^5/_8$ x 8 $^1/_2$ inches (29.5 x 21.6 centimeters).

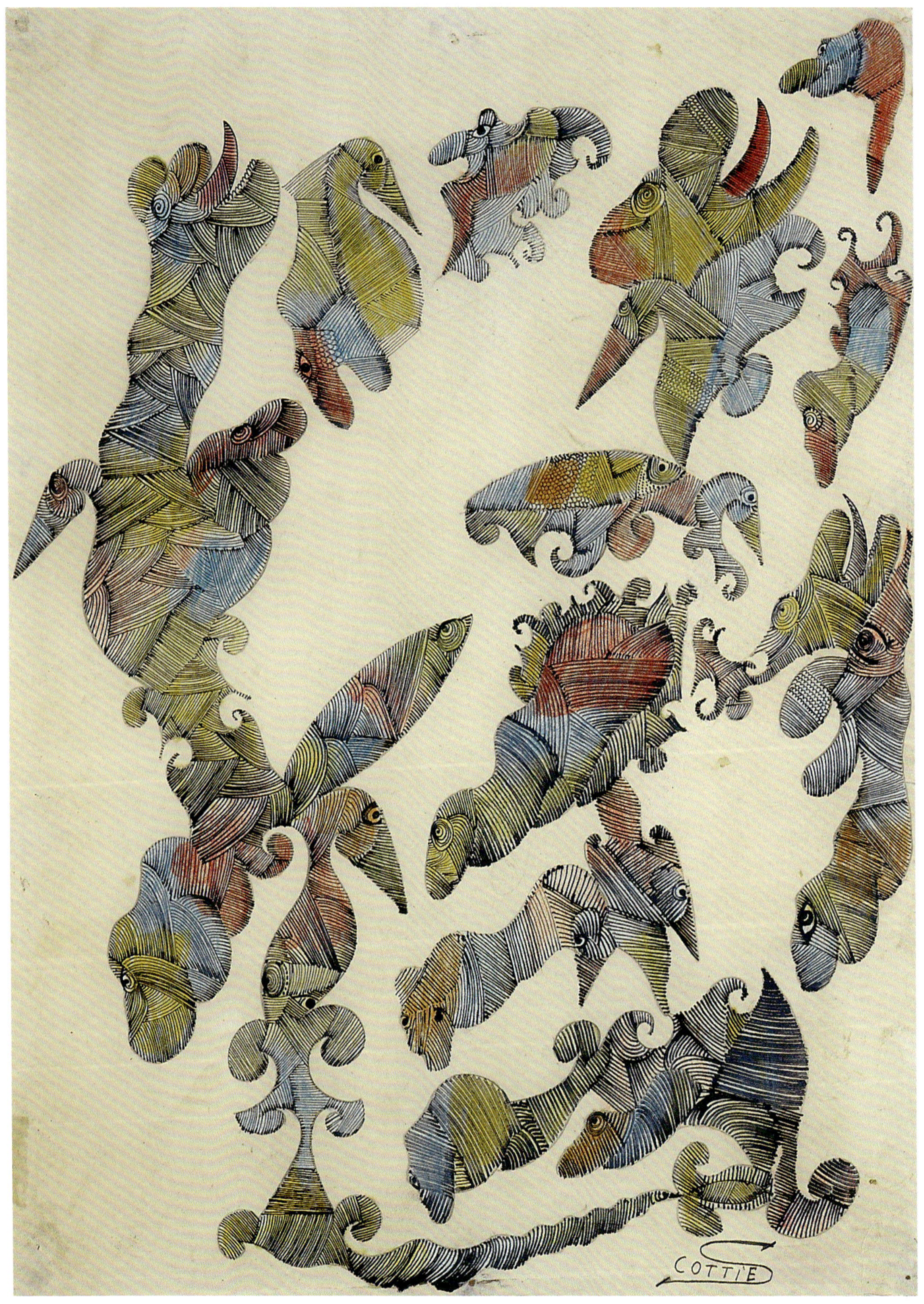

PLATE 4. *Herd of Greedies*, c. 1935. Pencil, colored pencil, and ink on paper. 15 x 11 inches (38.1 x 27.9 centimeters).

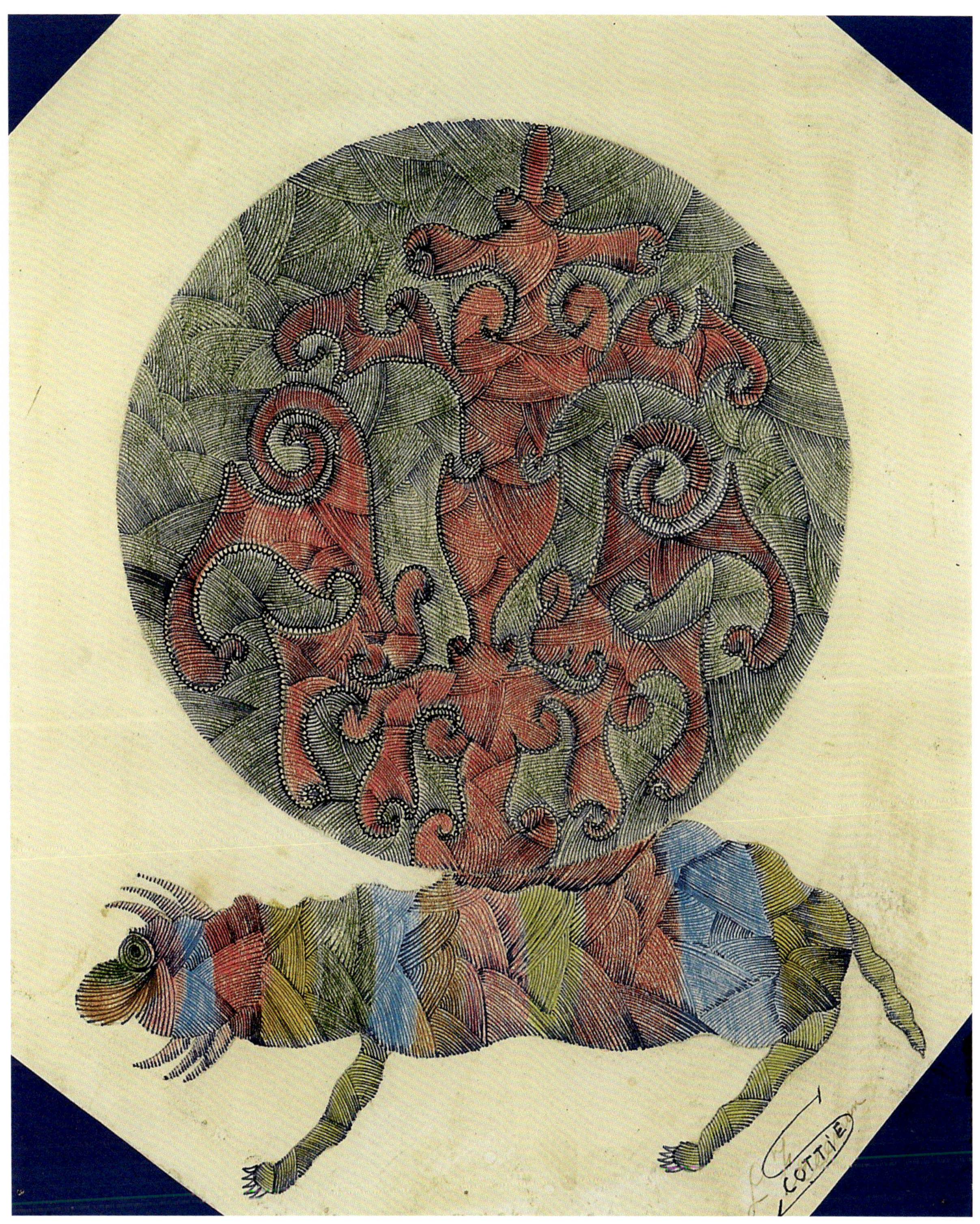

PLATE 5. *Animal and Globe (Atlas Greedy)*, c. 1935–40. Ink and crayon on paper. 13 x 10 $^{1}/_{2}$ inches (33 x 26.7 centimeters).

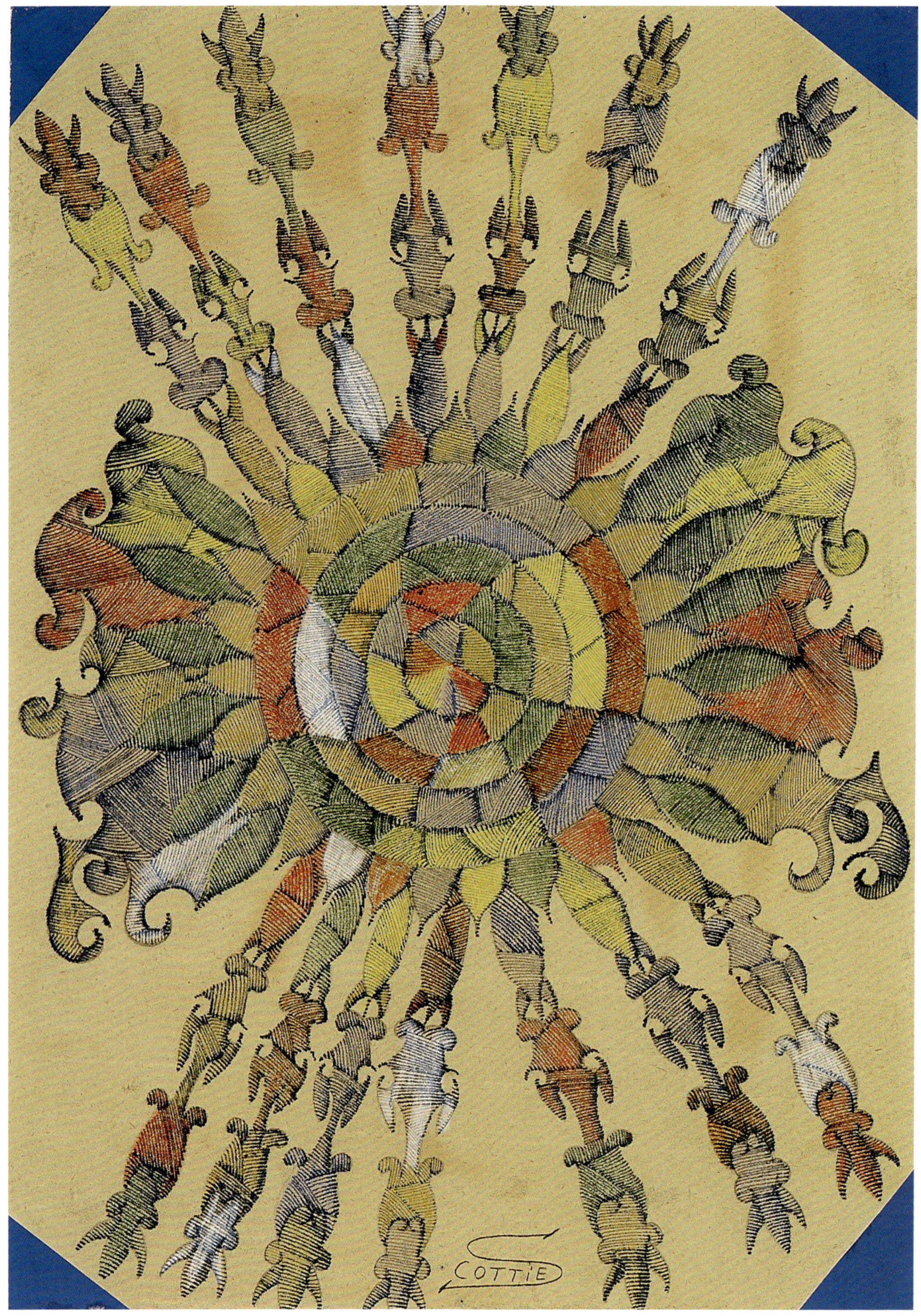

PLATE 6. *Pinwheel,* c. 1935–40. Pencil, colored pencil, and ink on paper. 15 x 10 inches (38.1 x 25.4 centimeters).

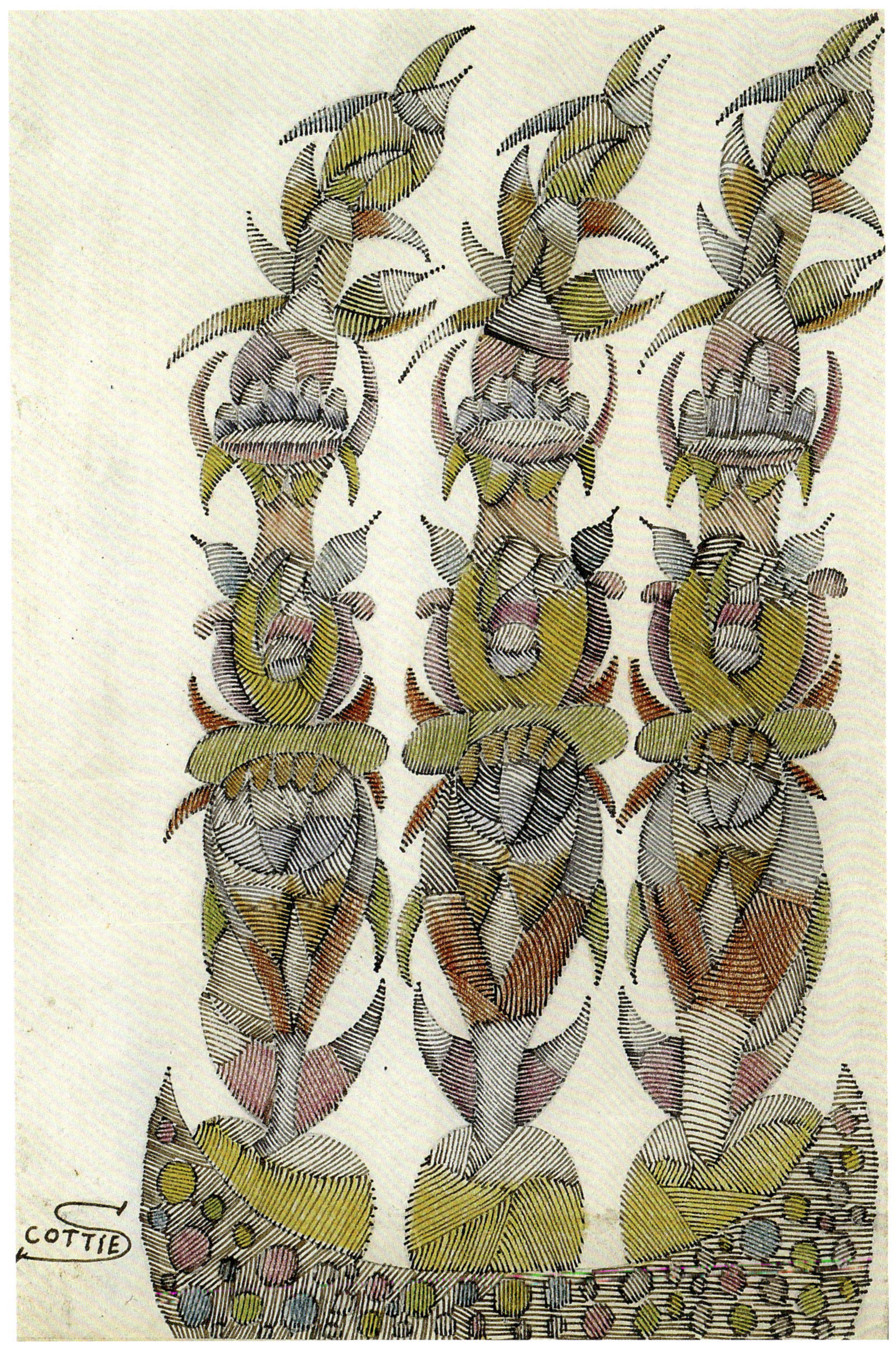

PLATE 7. *Sailing Totems*, c. 1935–42. Pencil, colored pencil, and ink on paper. 11 x 7 ¹⁄₂ inches (27.9 x 19.1 centimeters).

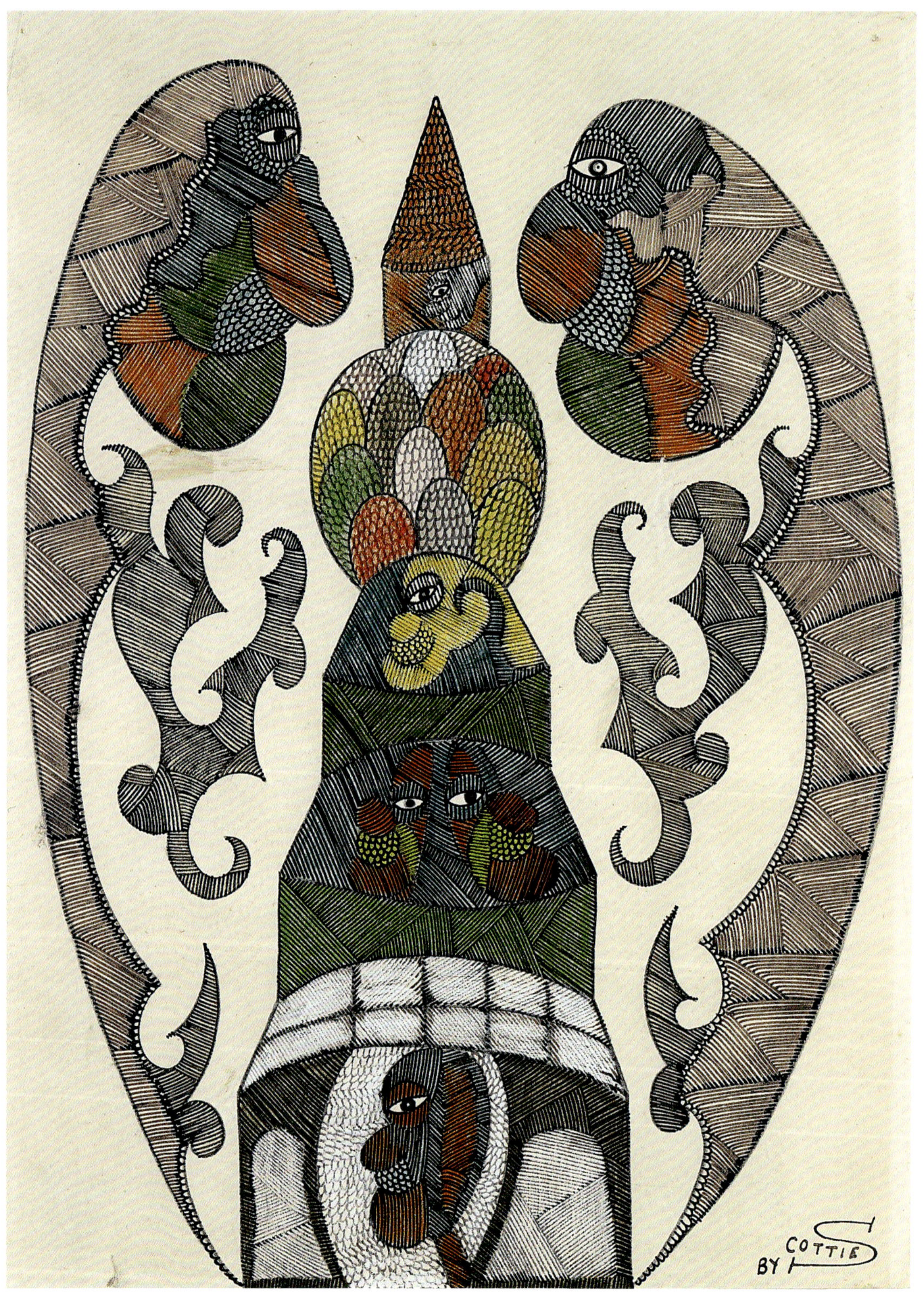

PLATE 8. *Temple of Light,* 1942. Colored pencil and ink on paper. 14 $^3/_4$ x 10 $^1/_2$ inches (37.5 x 26.7 centimeters).

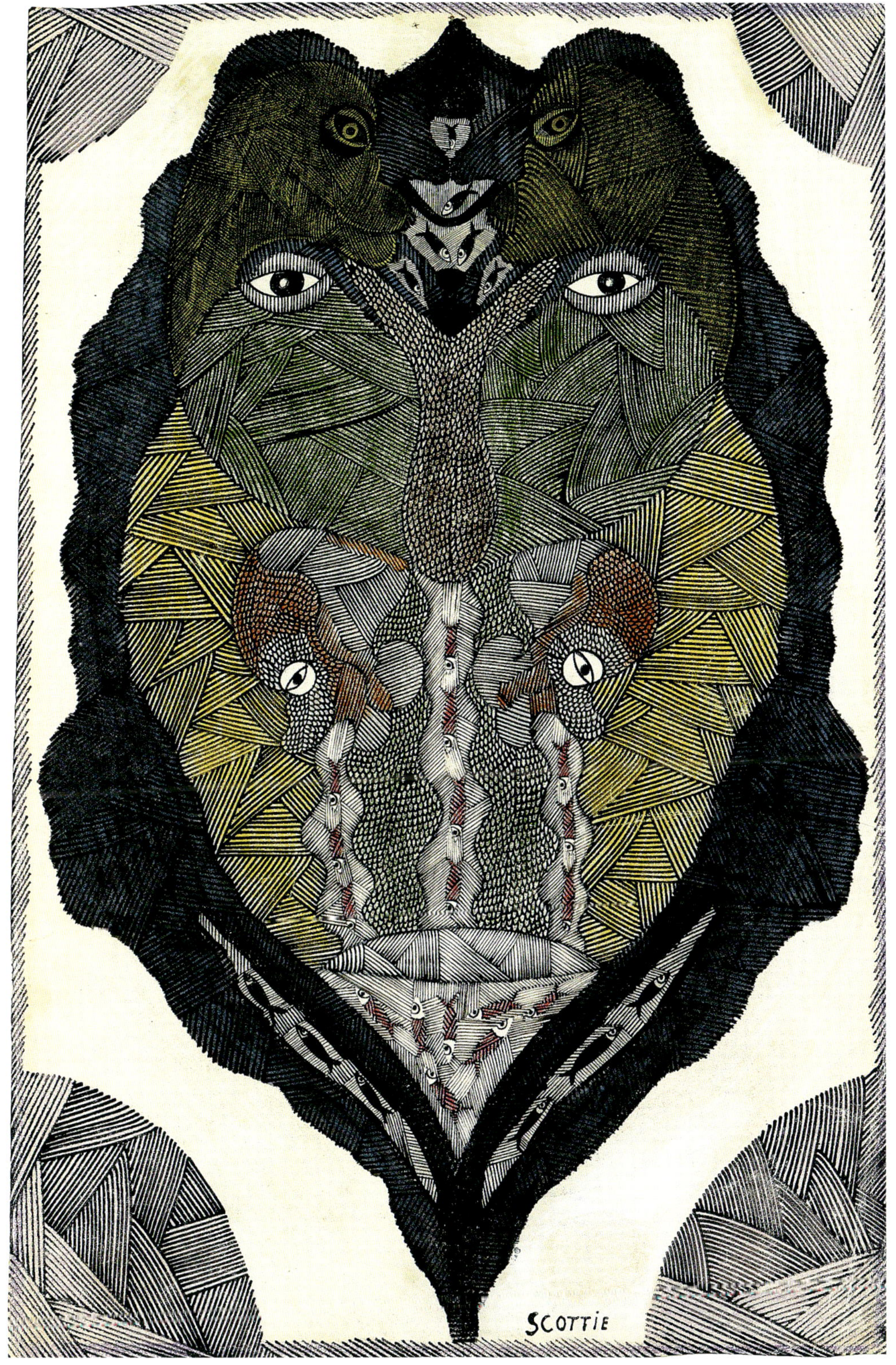

PLATE 9. *Black/Pink Fish and Faces,* c. 1942–50. Ink and crayon on paper. 16 5/8 x 11 inches (42.2 x 27.9 centimeters).

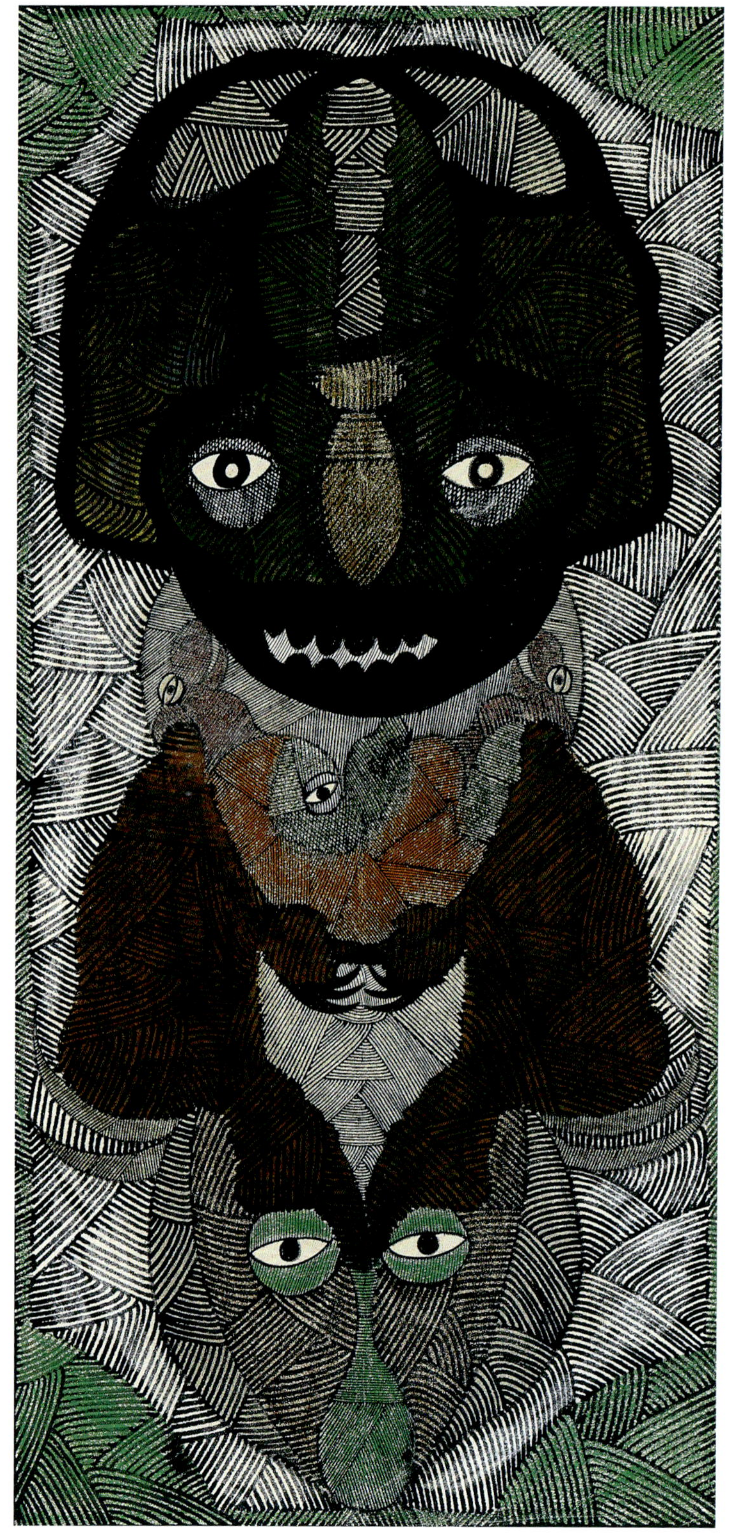

PLATE 10. *Green Brown Greedies,* c. 1946. Ink, crayon, and watercolor on paper. 17 x 9 $^{1}/_{2}$ inches (43.2 x 24.1 centimeters).

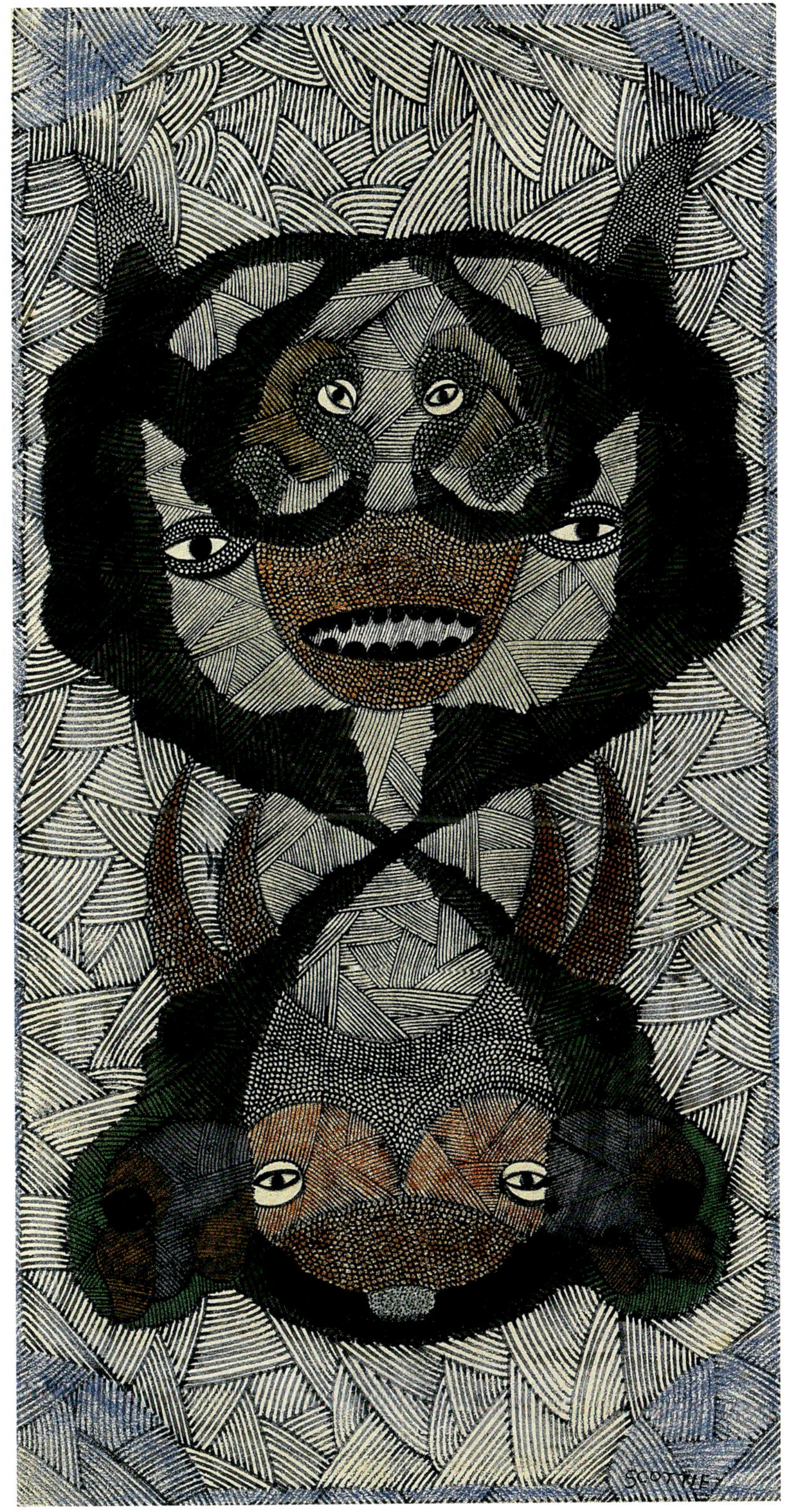

PLATE II. *Figure-8 Faces,* 1946. Crayon and watercolor on paper. 15 $\frac{1}{2}$ x 9 inches (39.4 x 22.9 centimeters).

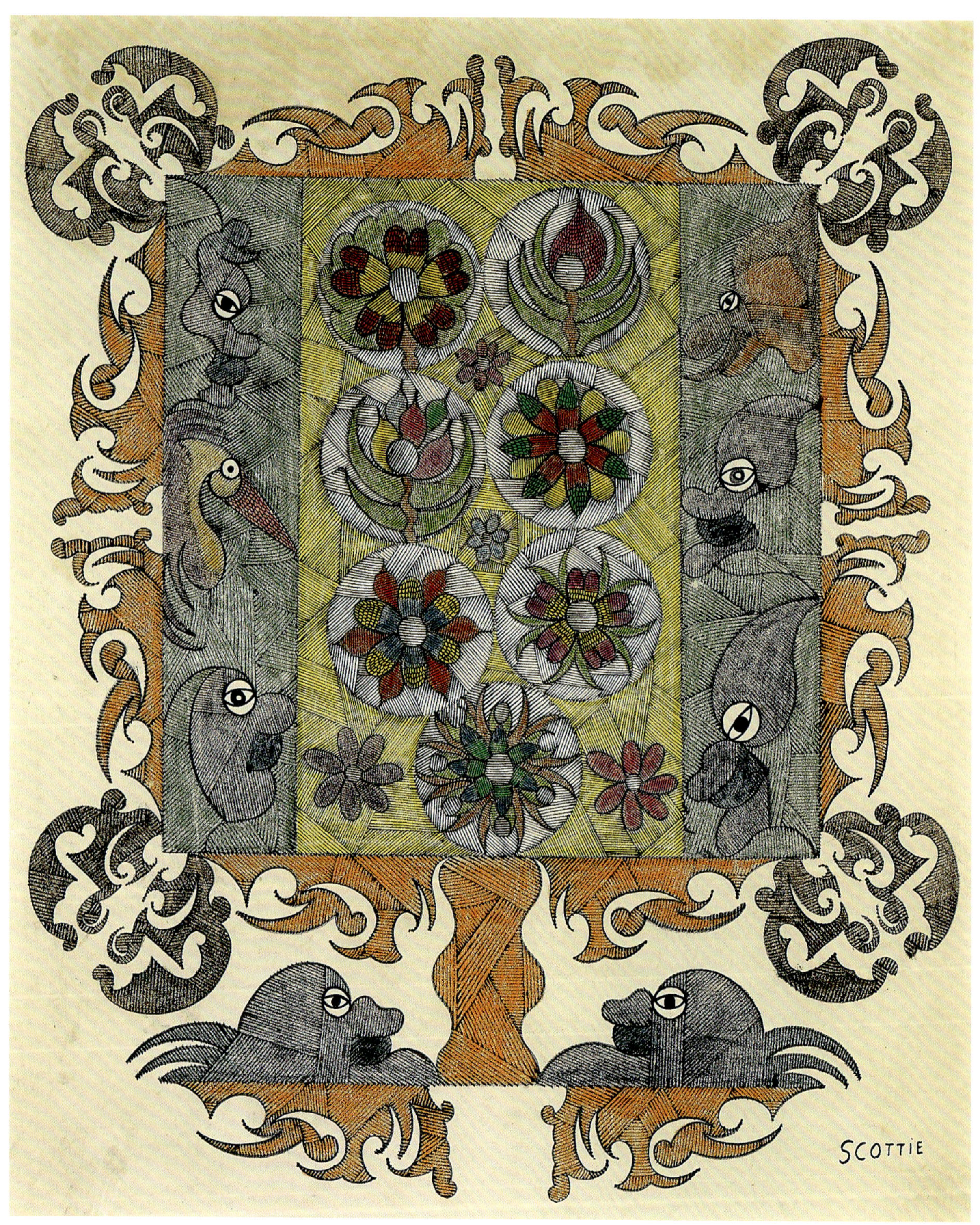

PLATE 12. *Square with Seven Circles,* c. 1950. Ink and crayon on paper. 22 x 19 inches (55.9 x 48.3 centimeters).

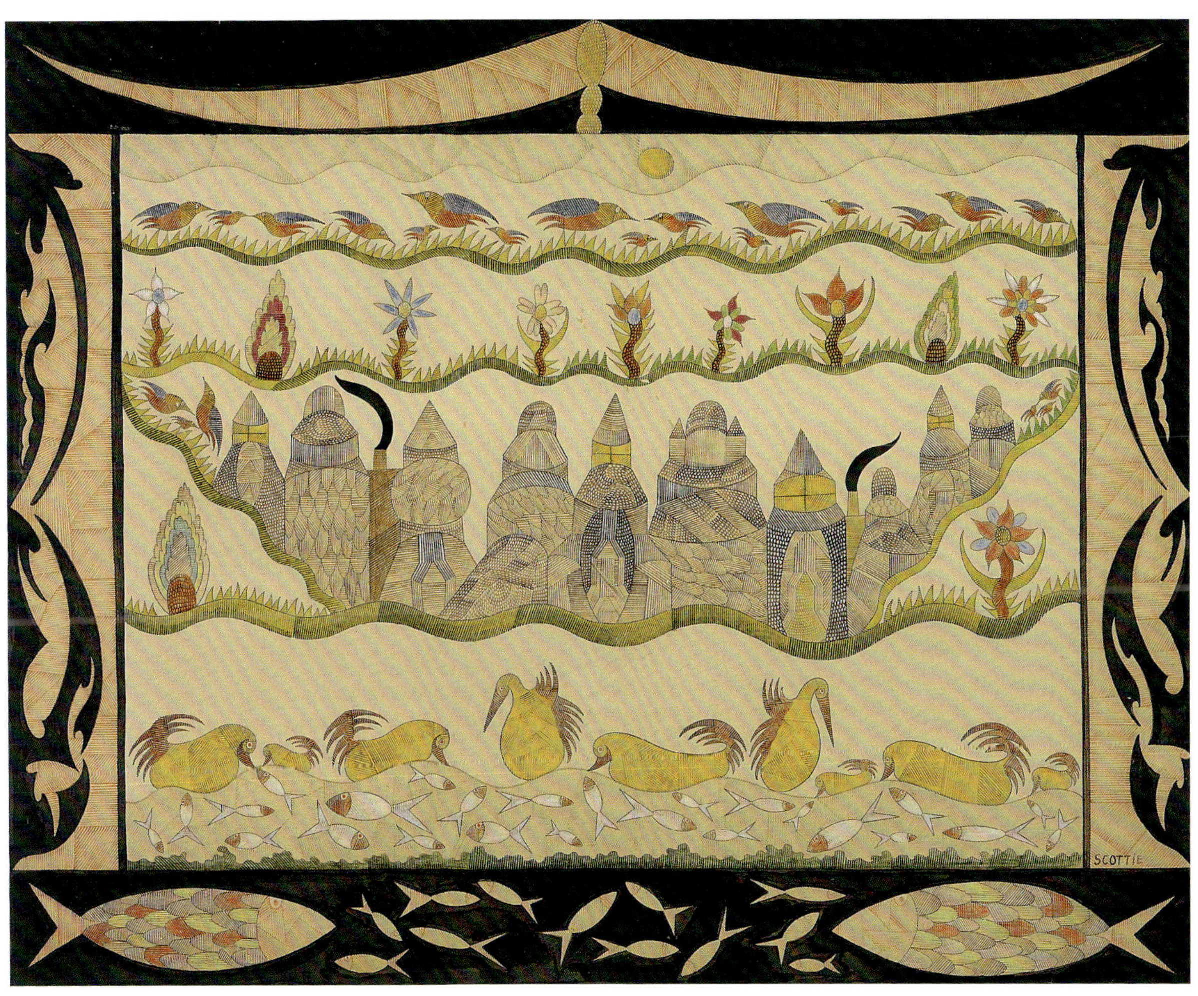

PLATE 13. *Spring.* c. 1960. Colored ink on paper. 26 $^3/_8$ x 33 $^1/_8$ inches (67 x 84.2 centimeters).

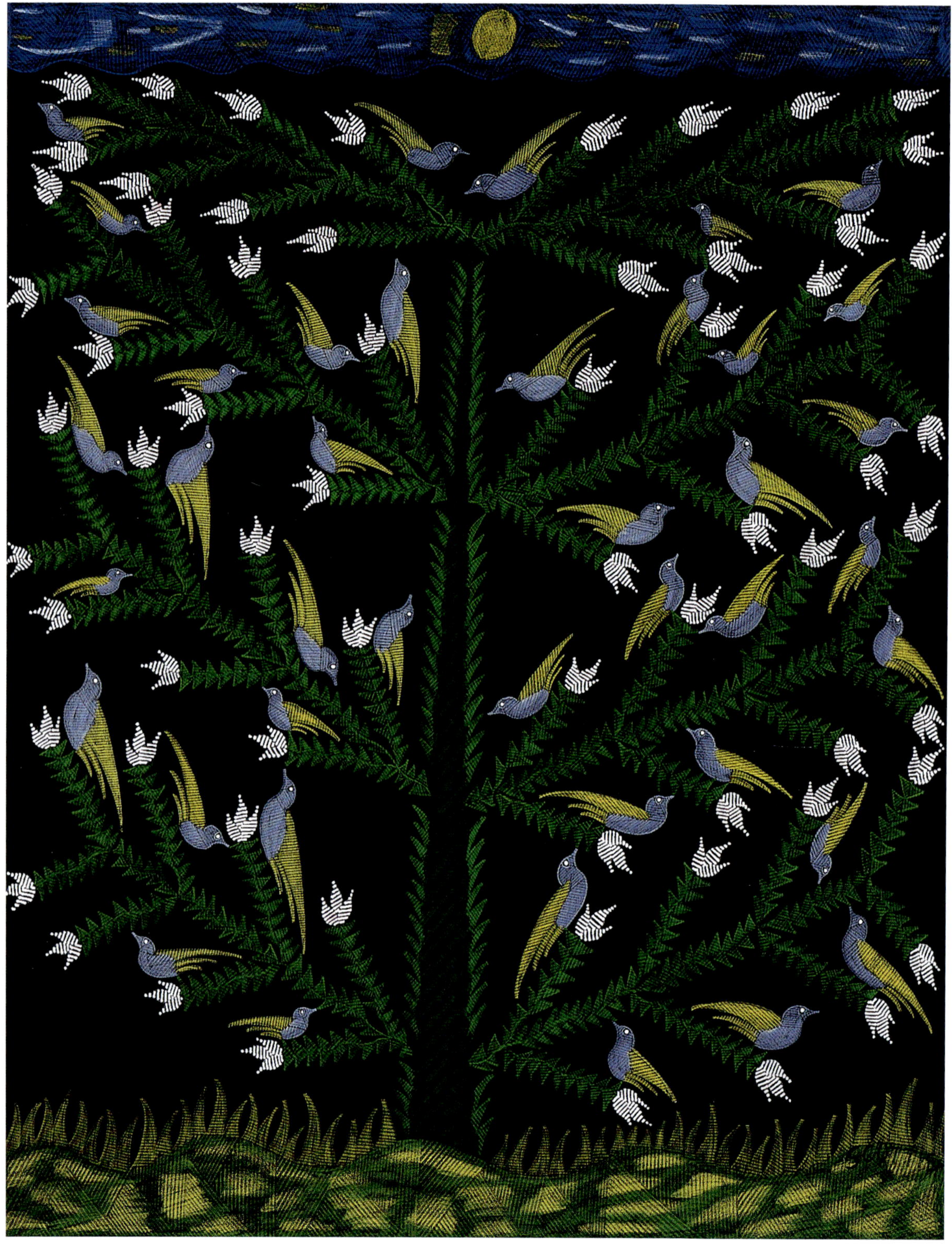

PLATE 14. *Blue Birds in the Tree*, c. 1960. Crayon and ink on paper. 25 5/8 x 20 1/2 inches (65.1 x 52.1 centimeters).

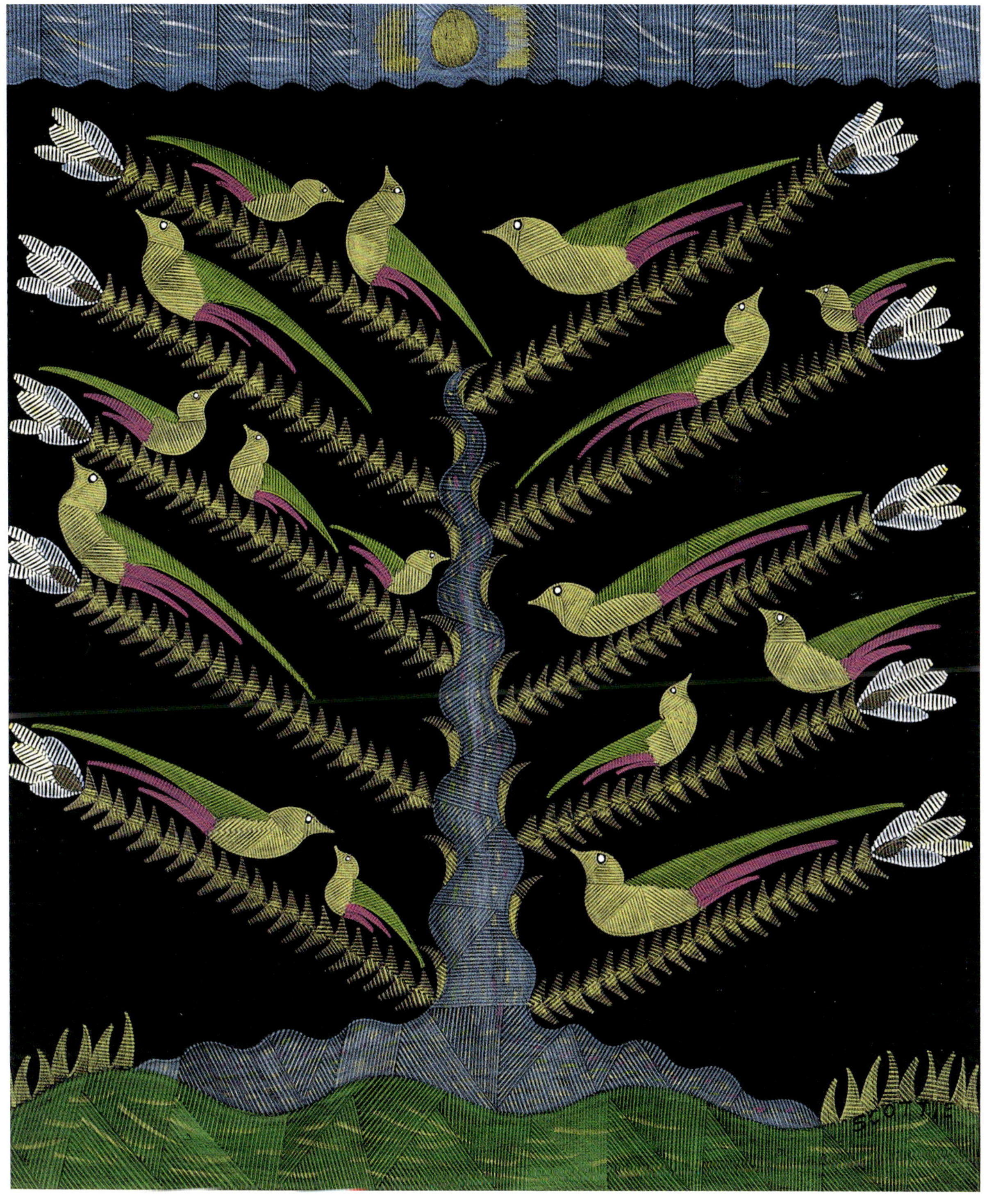

PLATE 15. *Yellow Birds in the Tree,* c. 1960. Ink and gouache on black paper. 23 $\frac{1}{2}$ x 20 inches (59.7 x 50.8 centimeters).

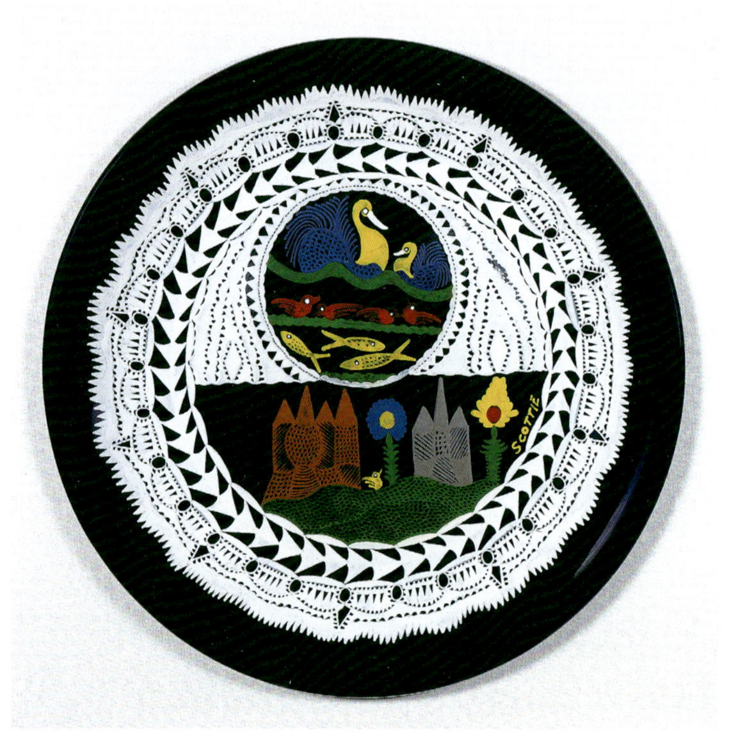

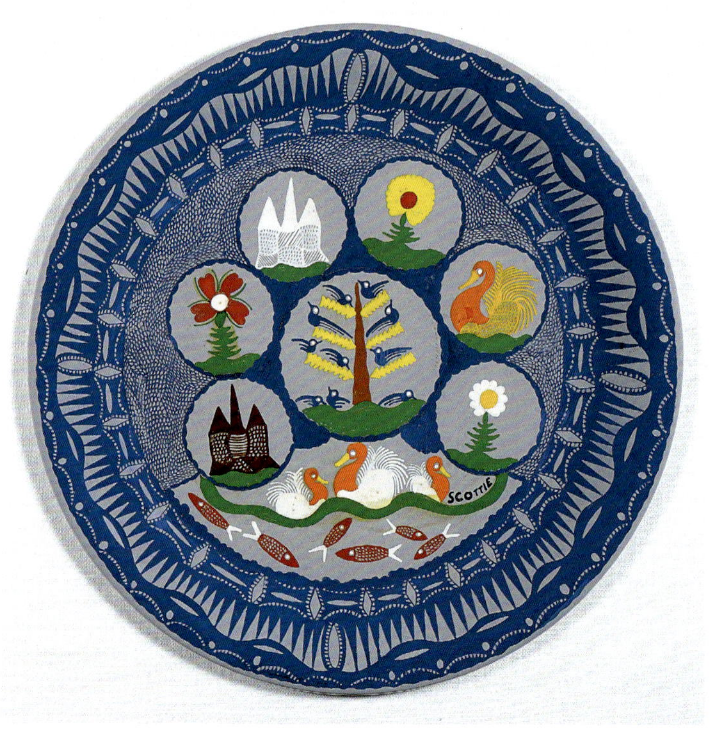

PLATE 16. *Hand–Painted Plates,* c. 1960.

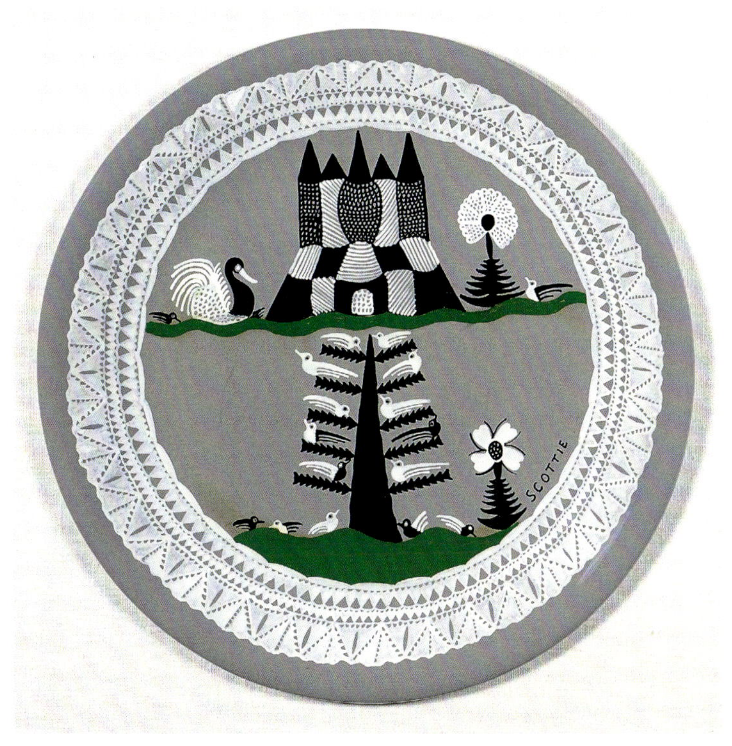

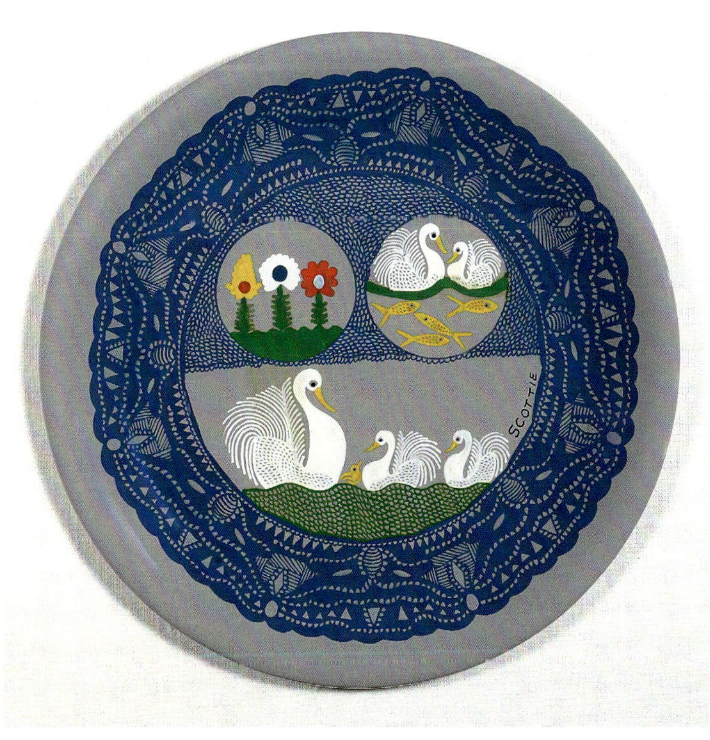

PLATE 17. *Hand-Painted Plates,* c. 1960.

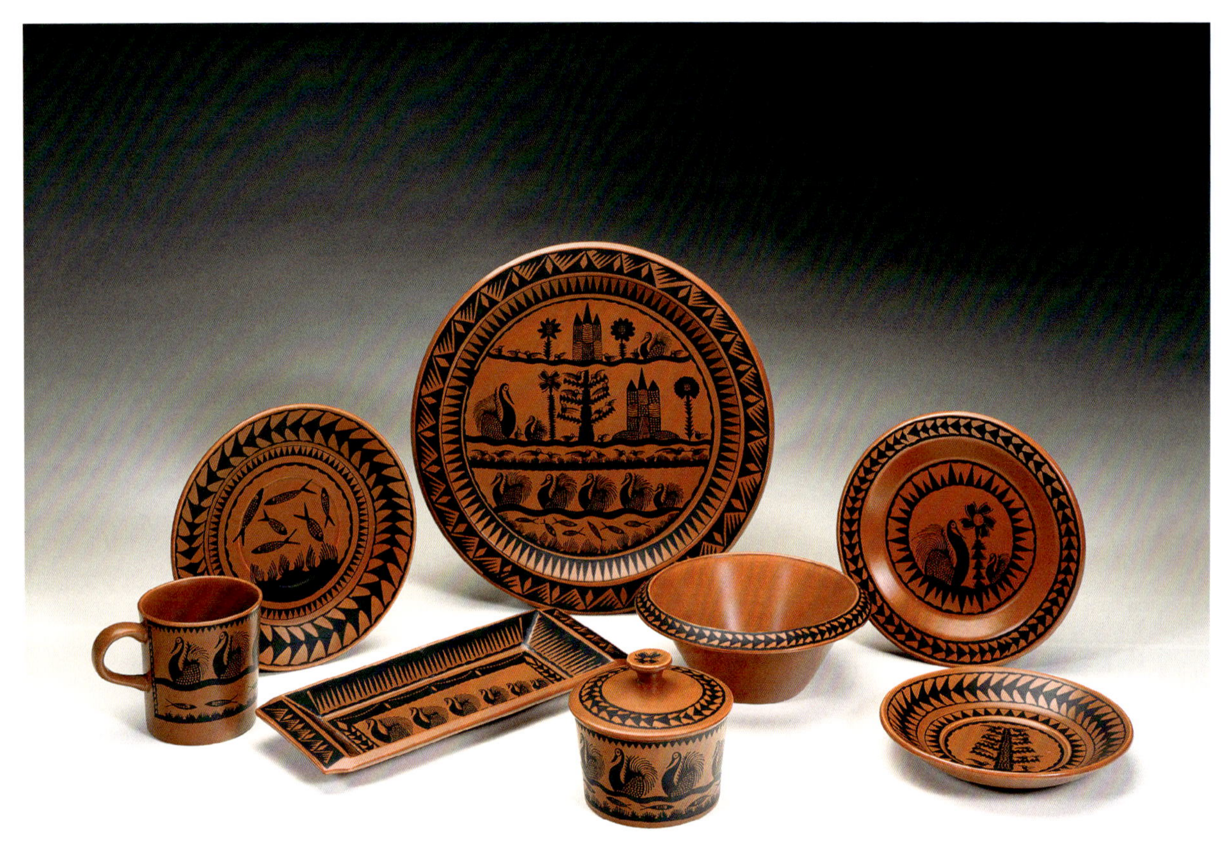

PLATE 18. Selection of Royal Worcester ceramics with design by Scottie Wilson.

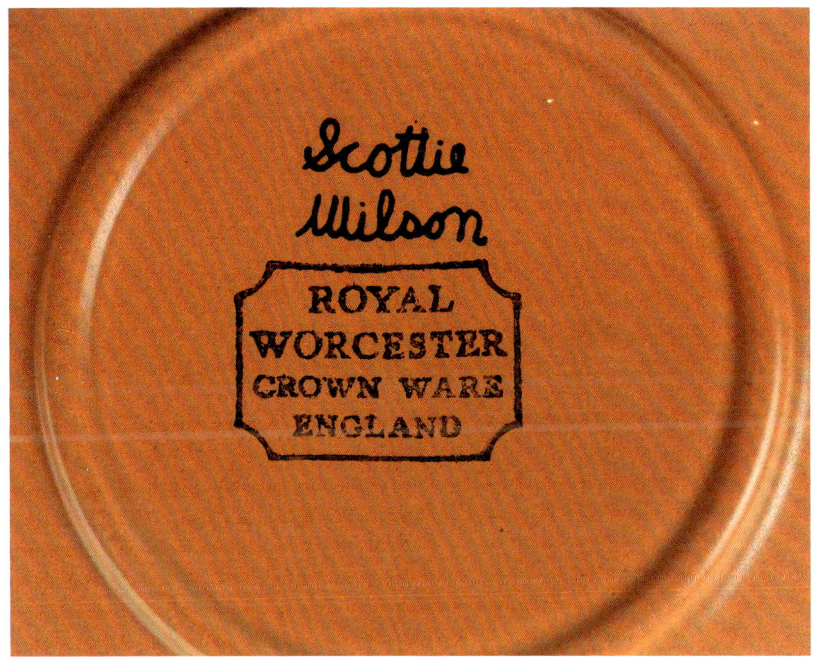

PLATE 19. Royal Worcester ceramics stamp with Scottie Wilson signature.

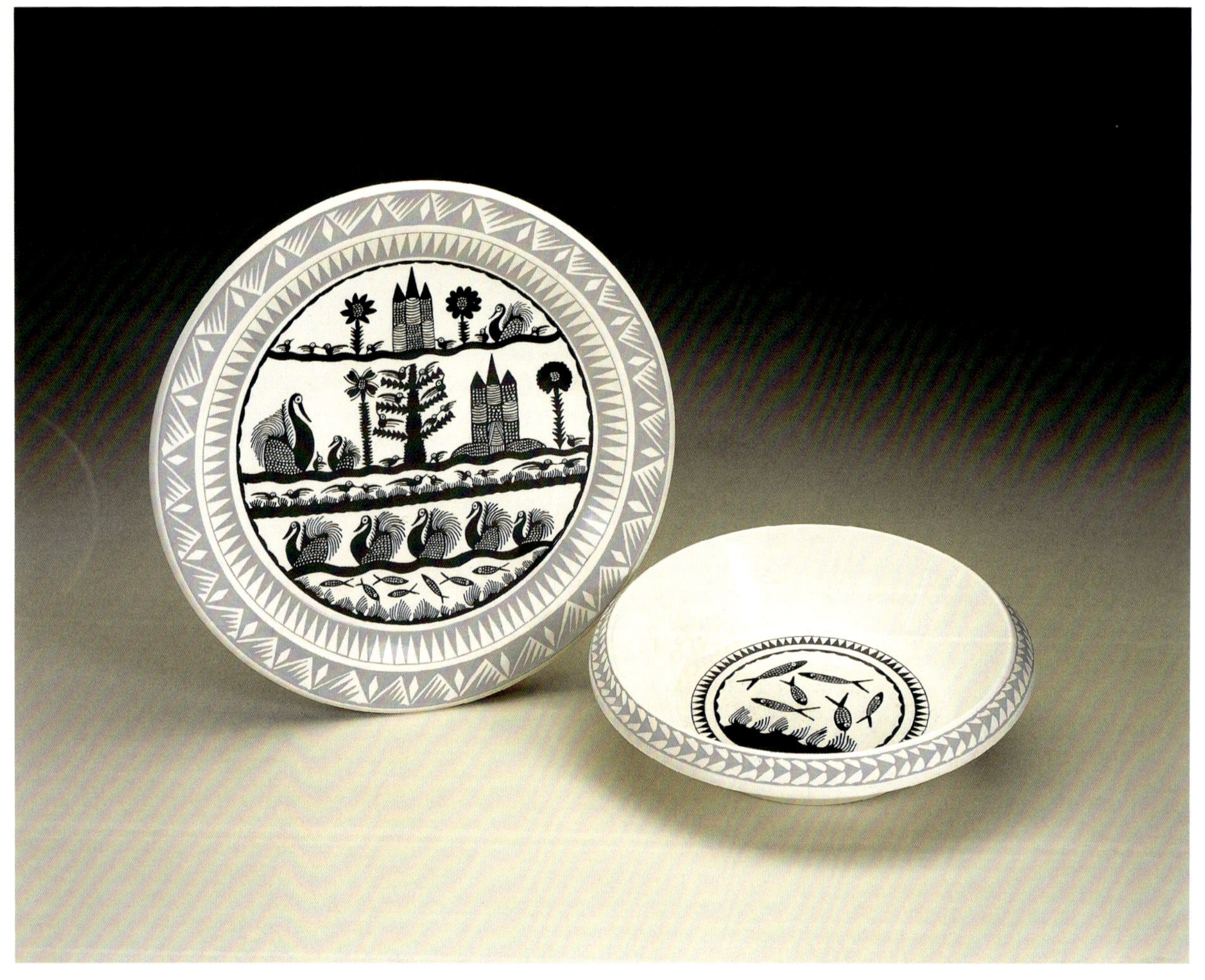

PLATE 20. Selection of Royal Worcester ceramics with design by Scottie Wilson.

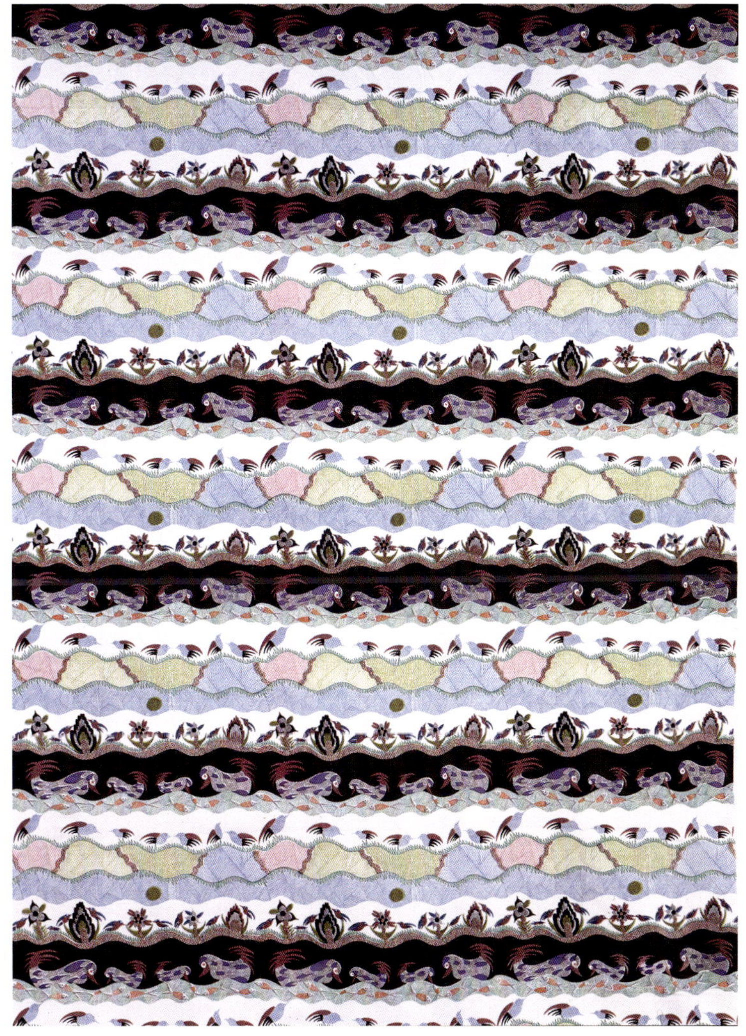

PLATE 21. *Textile with Design by Scottie Wilson*, Edinburgh Weavers textile. Courtesy of V&A Picture Library.

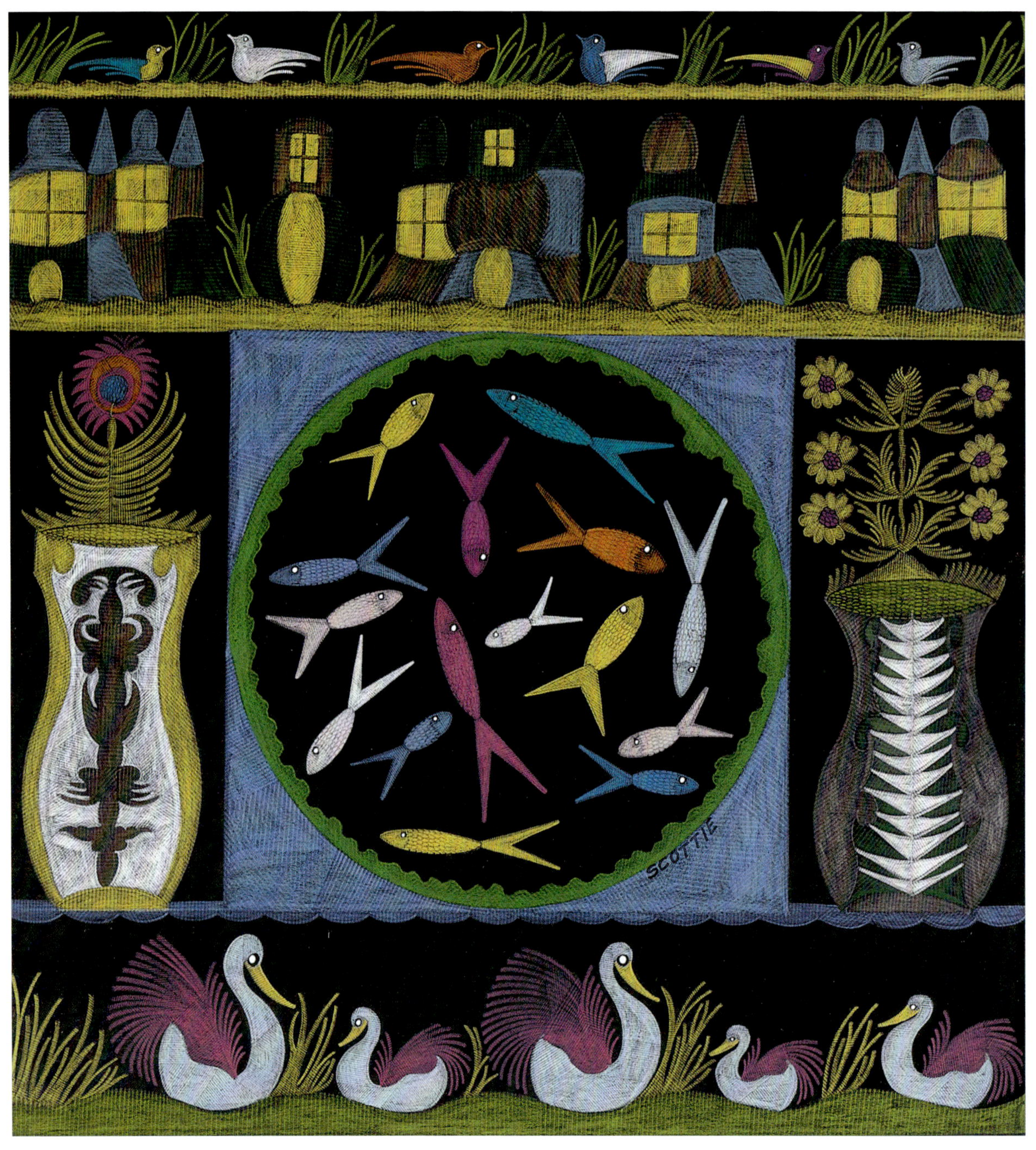

PLATE 22. *Center Fish Circle on Black,* c. 1965. Colored ink on paper. 14 $^3/_8$ x 10 $^7/_8$ inches (36.5 x 27.6 centimeters).

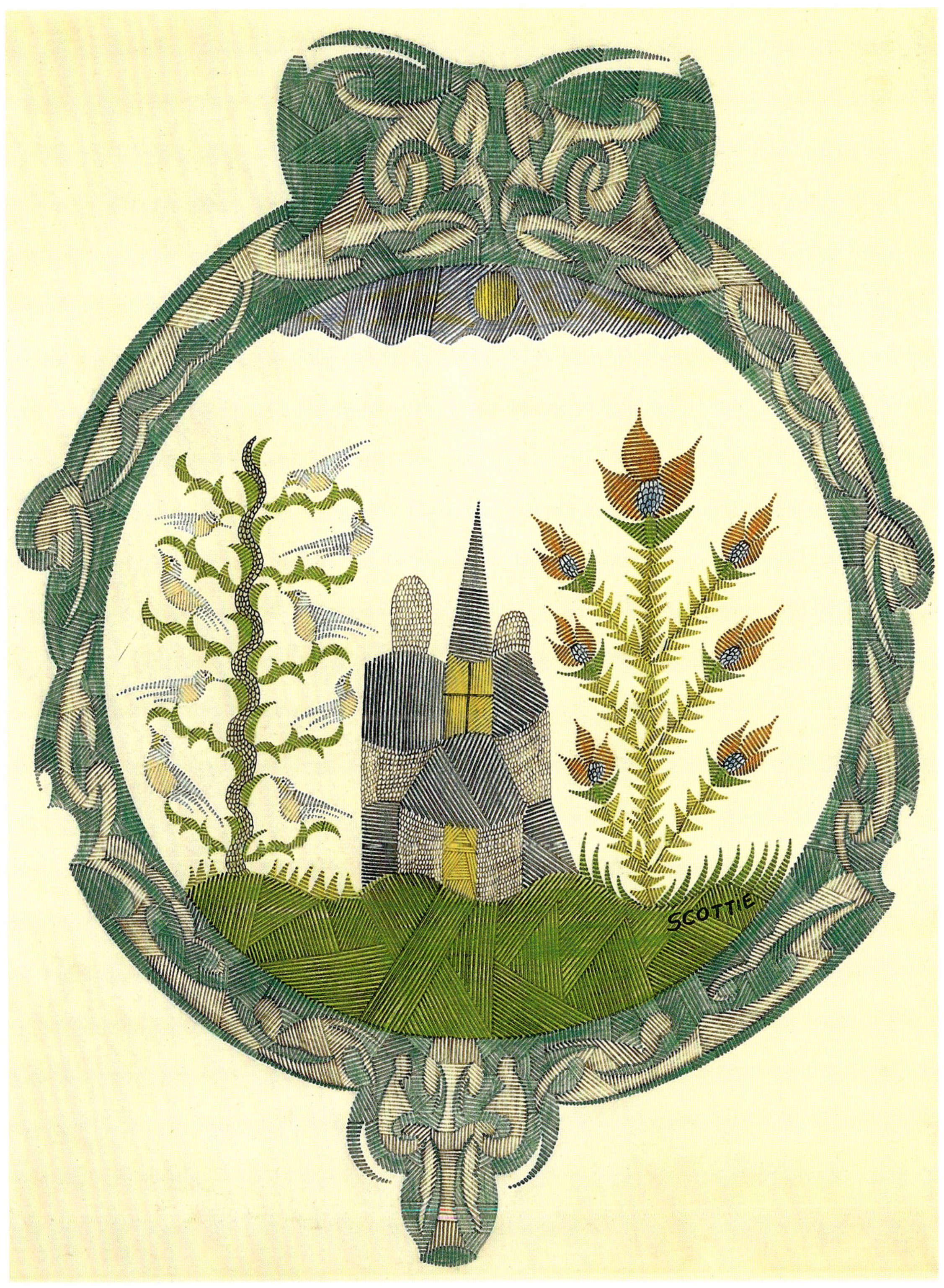

PLATE 23. *Magic Castle in the Mirror*, c. 1955. Colored ink on paper. 21 x 16 inches (53.3 x 40.6 centimeters).

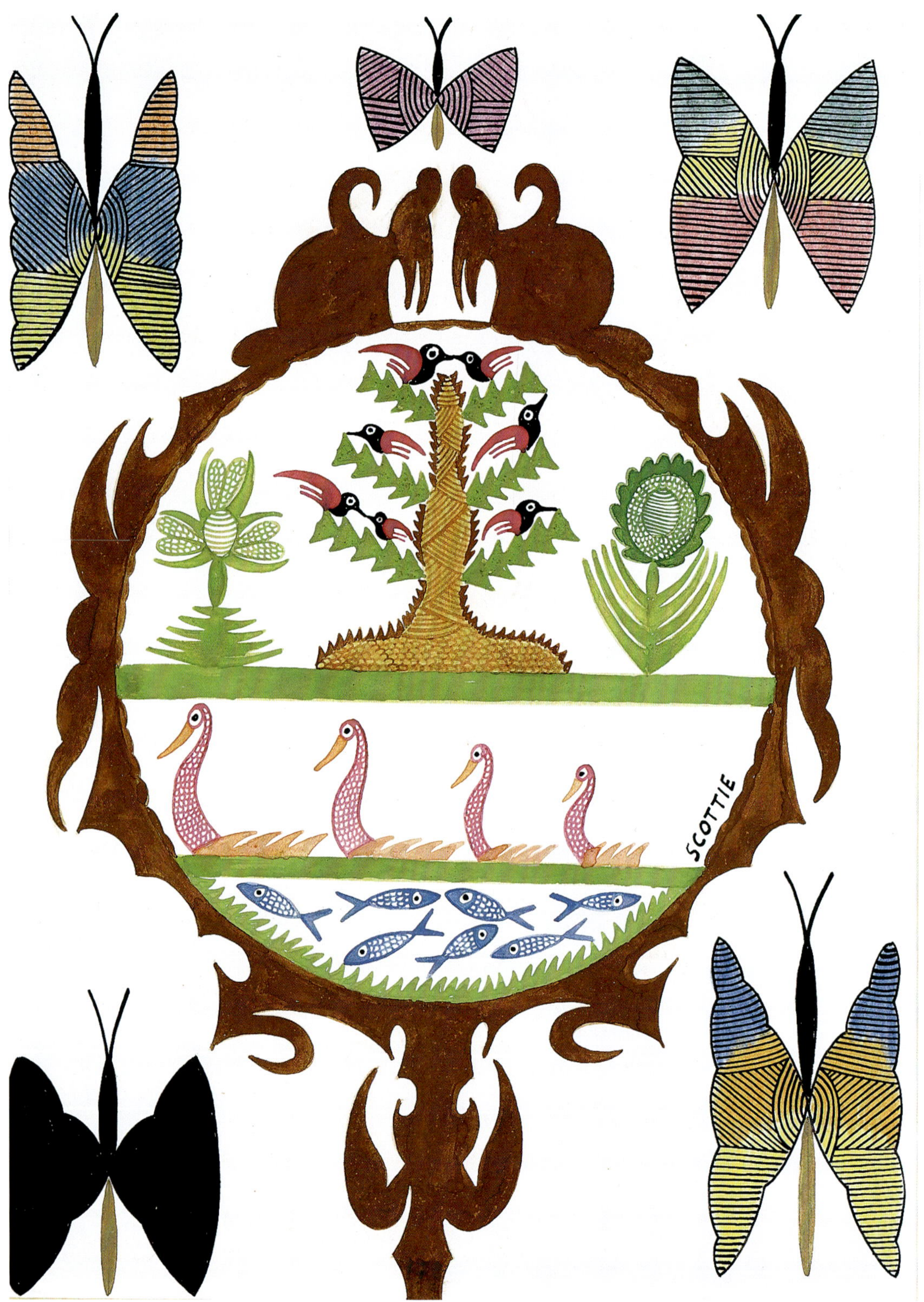

PLATE 24. *Five Butterflies*, c. 1965–72. Gouache, crayon, and watercolor on paper. 13 x 9 ³/₄ inches (33 x 24.8 centimeters).

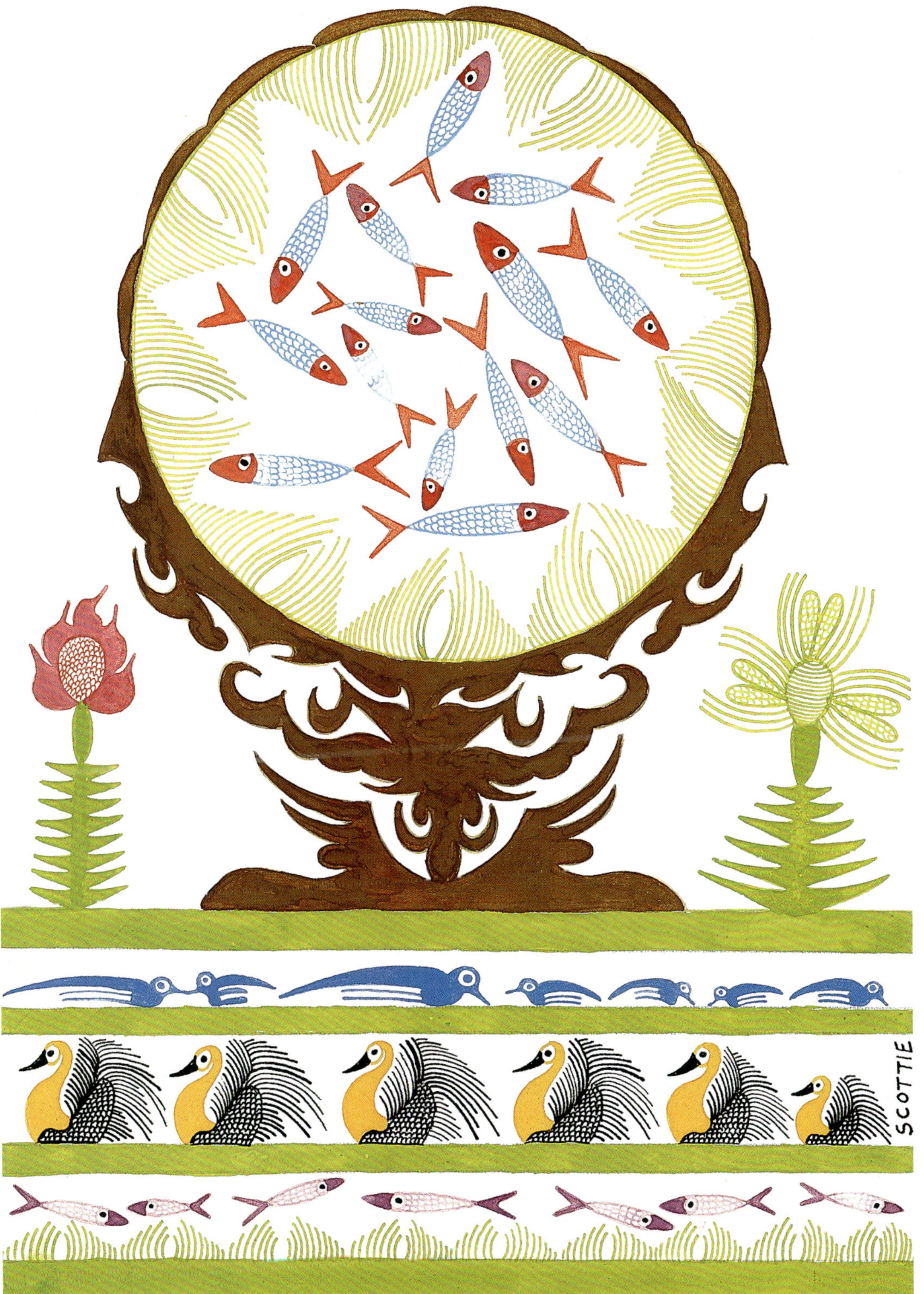

PLATE 25. *Red Fish Blue Fish in Brown Circle,* c. 1960–72. Watercolor, ink, and gouache on paper. 13 x 9 ³/₄ inches (33 x 24.8 centimeters).

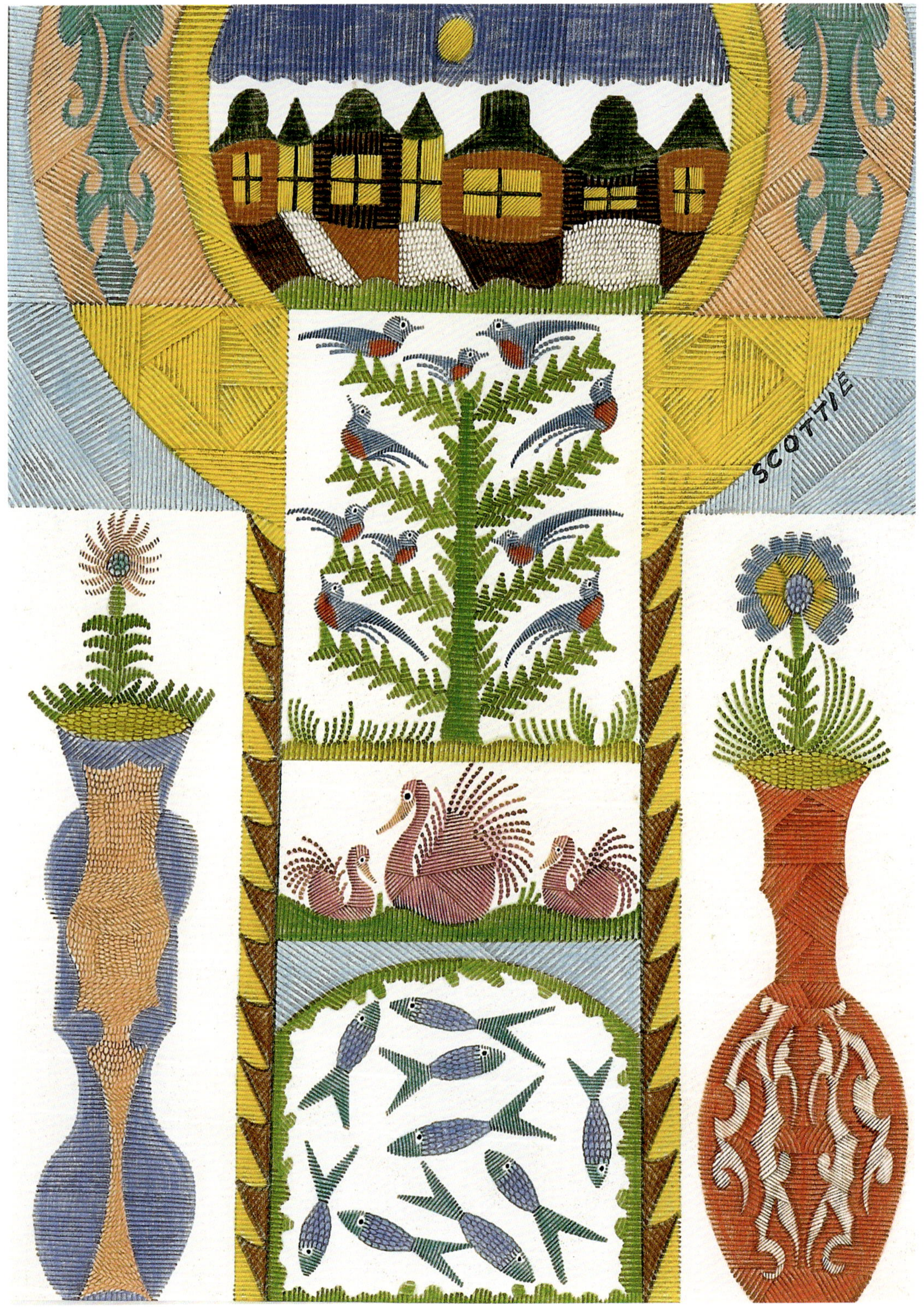

PLATE 26. *Red Vase*, c. 1960. Pencil, colored pencil, and ink on board. 23 $\frac{1}{2}$ x 20 inches (59.7 x 50.8 centimeters).

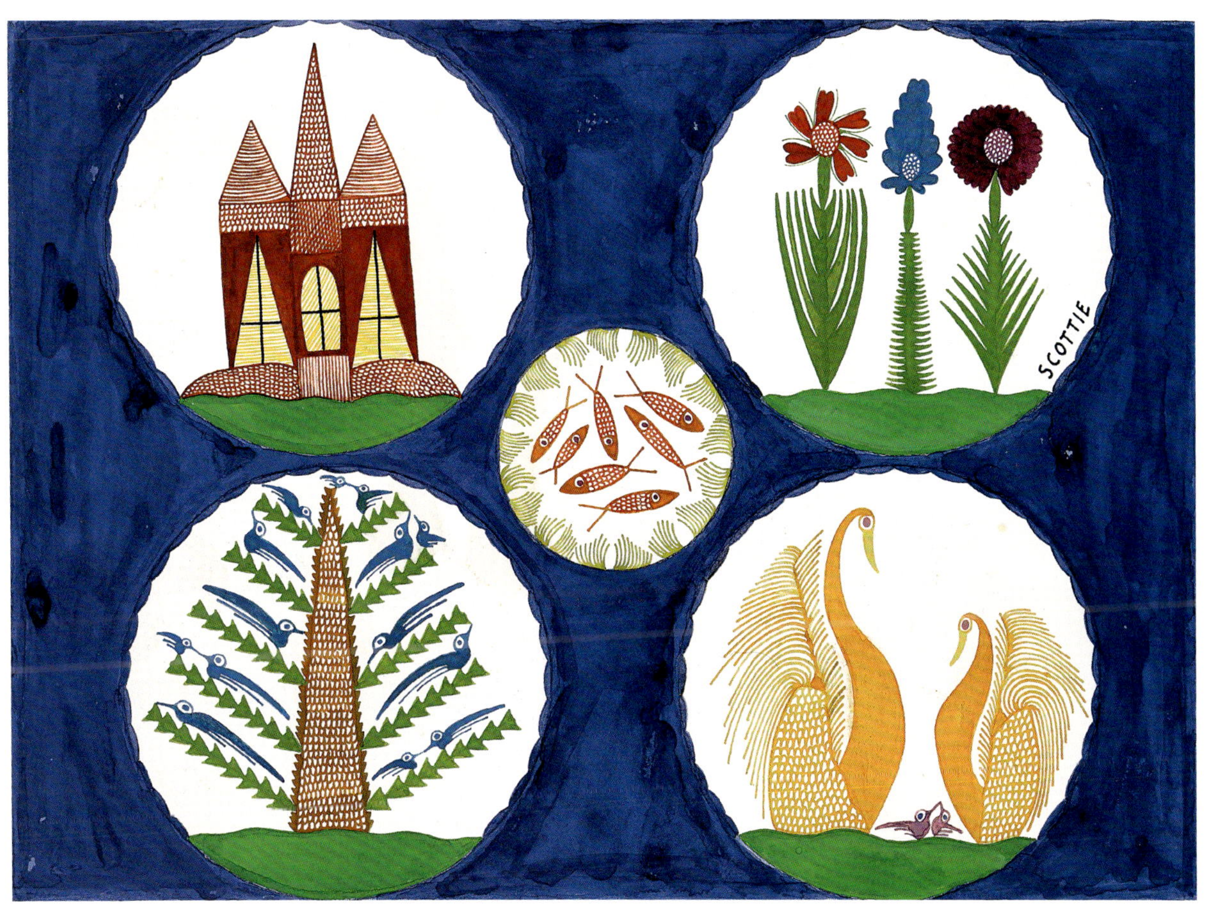

PLATE 27. *Five Circles on Blue*, c. 1965–72. Gouache on paper. 10 ¹⁄₄ x 14 ³⁄₄ inches (26 x 37.5 centimeters).

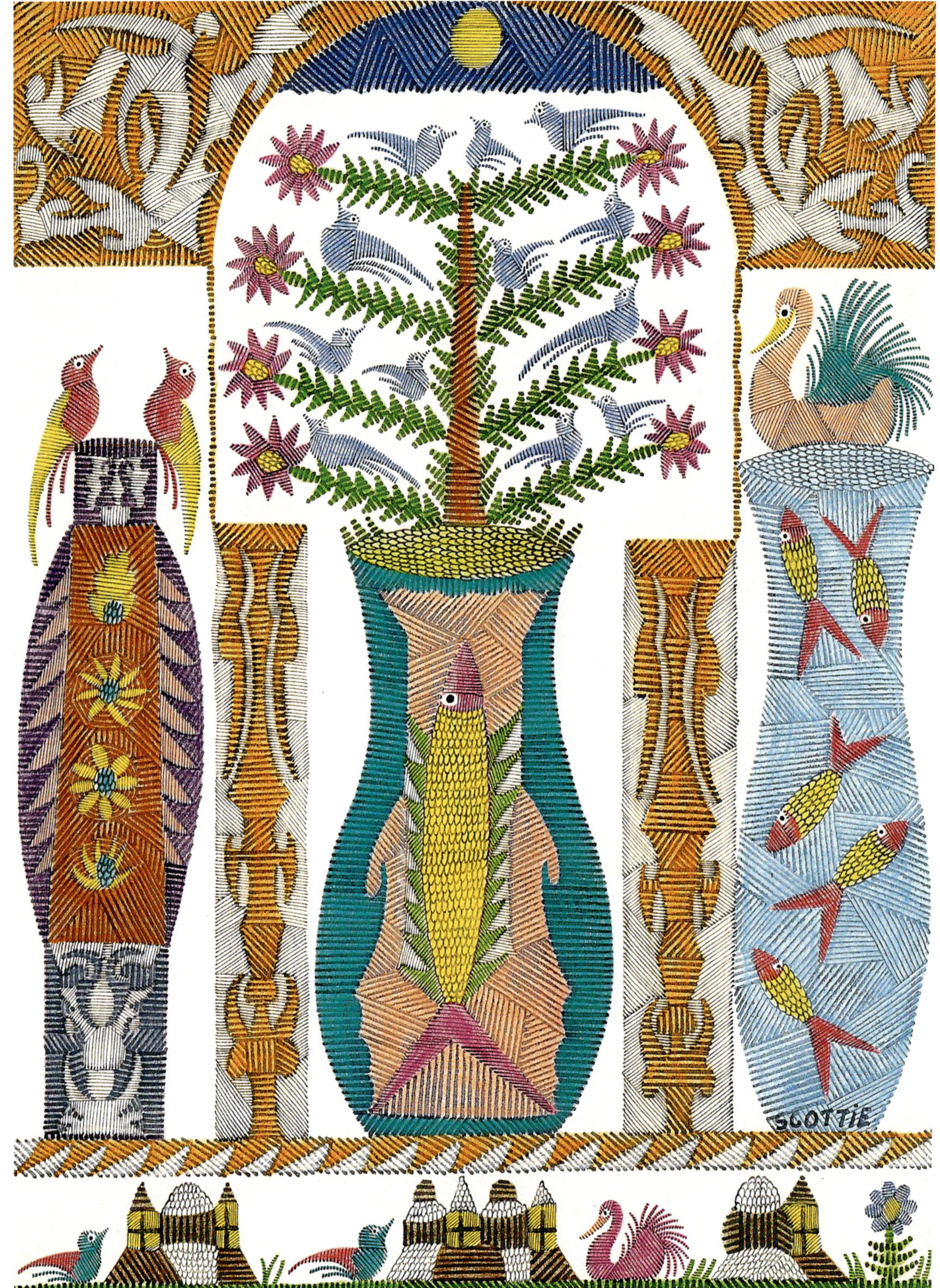

PLATE 28. *Three Vases*, c. 1955–65. Ink on board. 14 $^{15}/_{16}$ x 11 $^{1}/_{4}$ inches (37.9 x 28.6 centimeters).

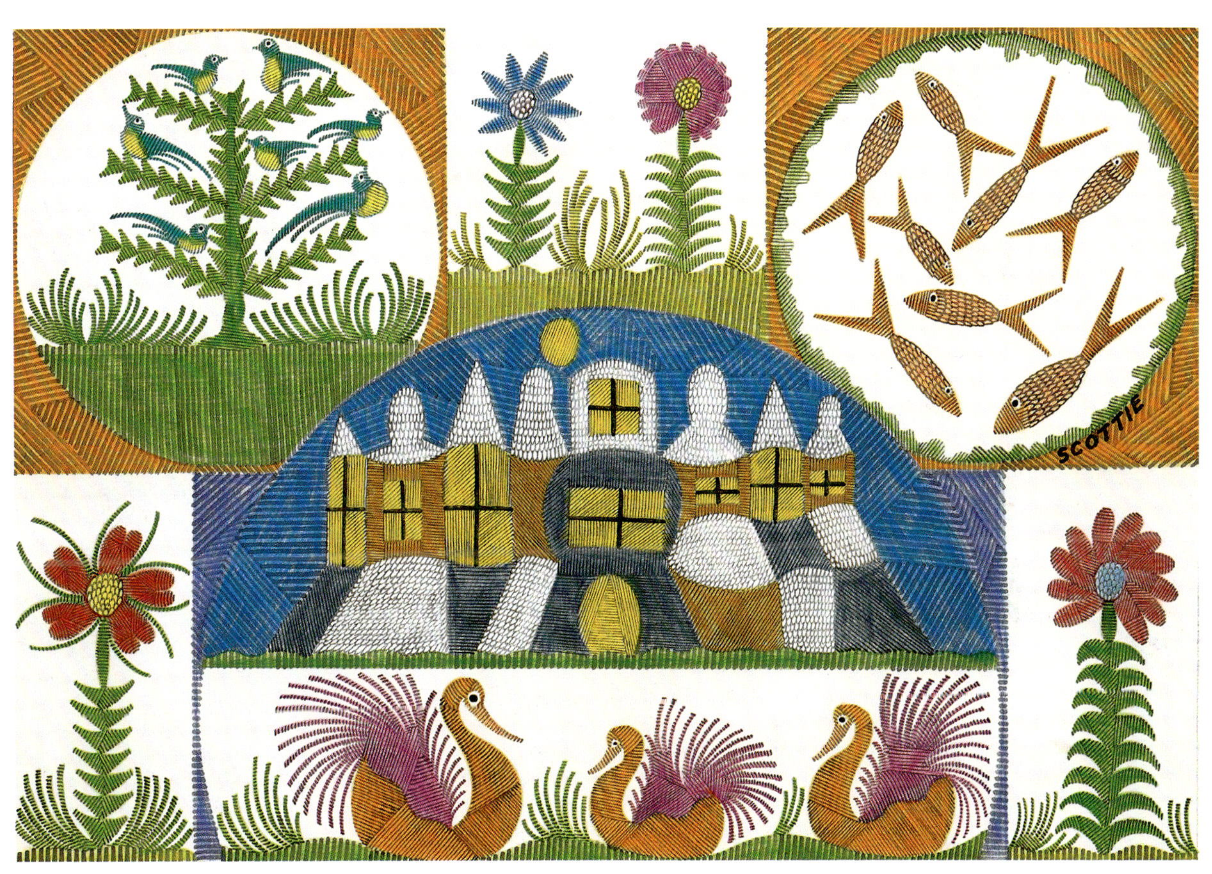

PLATE 29. *Orange and Purple Swans,* c. 1955–65. Ink on board. 10 $^{7}/_{16}$ x 15 inches (26.5 x 38.1 centimeters).

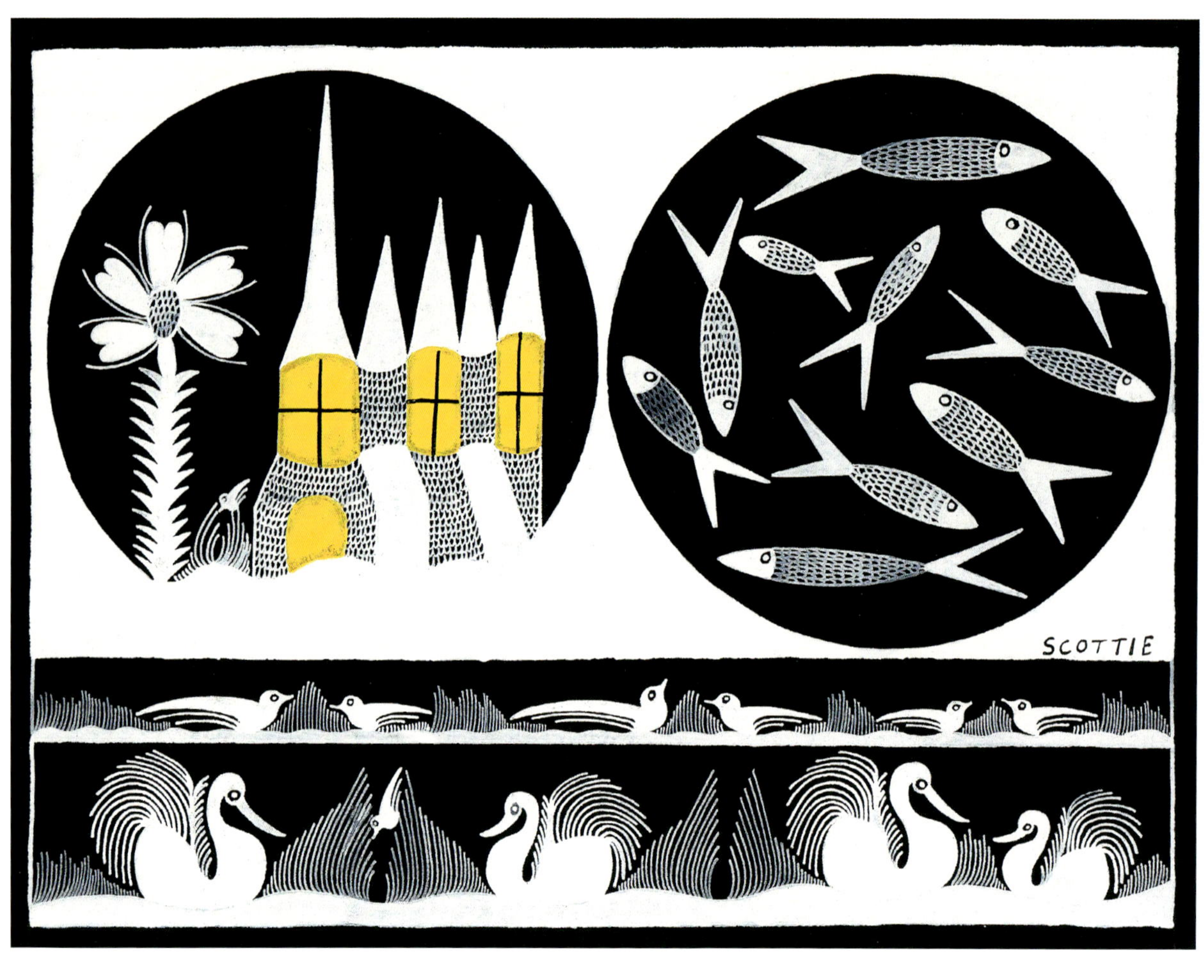

PLATE 30. *Black and White with Yellow Windows,* c. 1965–72. Gouache and ink on board. 9 ¹⁵/₁₆ x 12 ½ inches (25.2 x 31.8 centimeters).

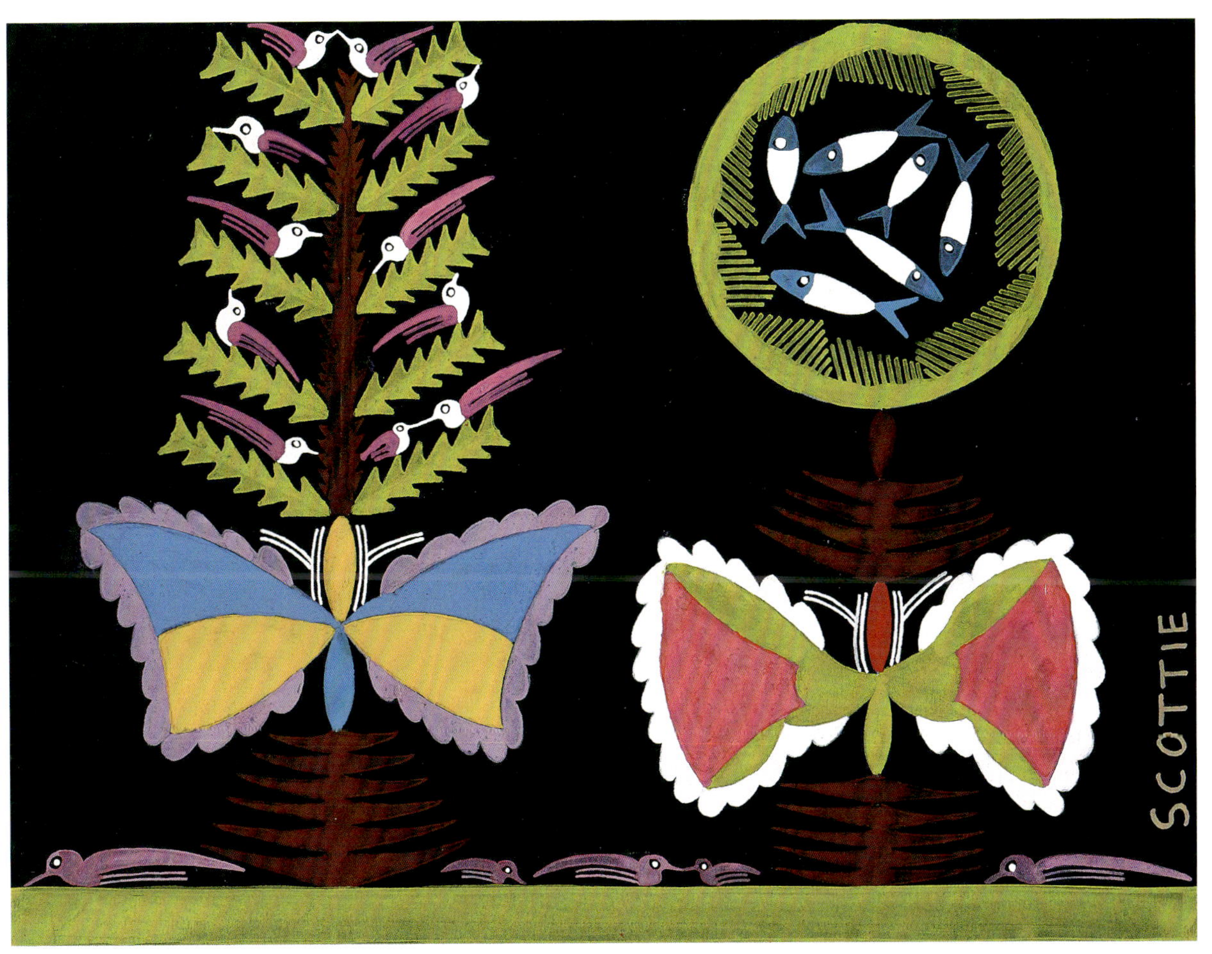

PLATE 31. *Butterfly Palace II,* c. 1965–72. Gouache on paper. 10 $^1/_4$ x 13 $^3/_4$ inches (26 x 34.9 centimeters).

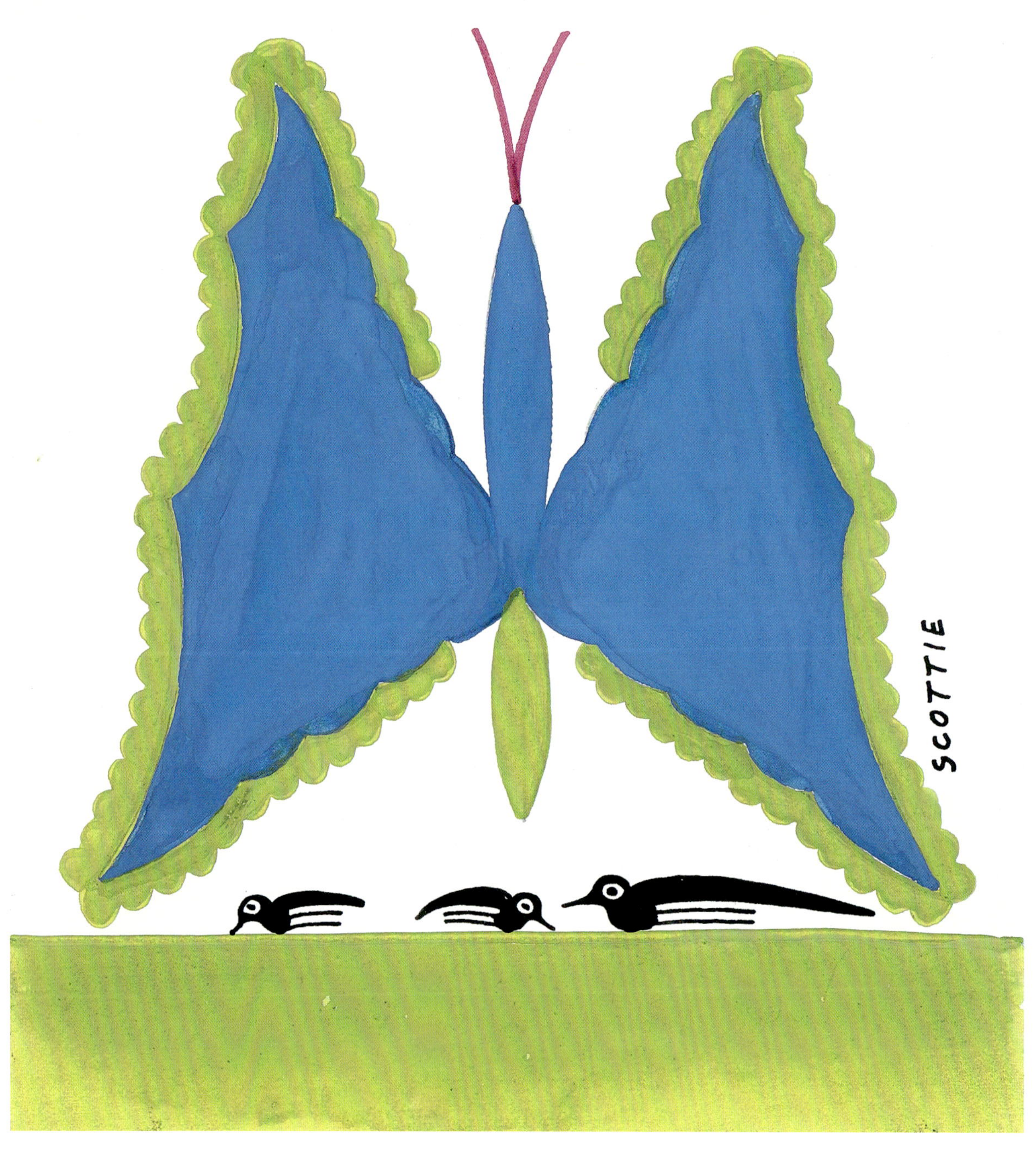

PLATE 32. *Big Blue Butterfly*, c. 1971. Gouache on cardboard. 7 x 6 inches (17.8 x 15.2 centimeters).

his upbringing in the Gorbals section of Glasgow. He wore glasses, which became thicker as the years went on, and maintained a taste for candy, whiskey, and kippers. It was not uncommon for him to have some sort of treat with him, and he would frequently offer to share with people he met.

He was an odd, evasive character. He held a deep mistrust and distaste for politicians and intellectuals, whom he found insincere and full of hot air. Mouthpieces, he called them disparagingly. Scottie had no interest in their convoluted opinions or personal agendas; he may have been lacking in formal education, but he was certainly keen, resourceful, and an acute observer of the world he lived in.

There were some other peculiar habits Scottie clung to. Whereas he could be quite generous with the odd piece of candy or kipper, he was something of a tightwad when it came to money. Never flashy or ostentatious, Scottie was quite prudent, but did not dispel the notion that he was a bit "down on his luck" and could usually use a few pounds or so. Duncan had given him a considerable sum to finance his return to England, but soon after arriving, Scottie asked his nephew Alan Freeman for a loan of three hundred pounds, which he said he would return "when his money came through." It's unclear what this statement meant and what money he was expecting, but this was a sum several times what he had borrowed from Duncan. Perhaps he was going to repay Duncan with the new loan, and he would soon be making money from the sale of his art. Whatever his intention, he never repaid his nephew.[78] A similar episode happened when Scottie visited his nephew Morris and his wife, Betty, at Leigh-on-Sea; he borrowed money from them and never repaid it.[79] This nasty habit of borrowing money, needed or not, and failing to repay the lender may explain why Scottie had so little contact with family members later in his life.

Scottie did occasionally send small amounts of money to his oldest sibling, Philip, the father of Alan Freeman. In an April 12, 1966, letter to Scottie, his brother wrote:

> *Sorry to hear that you are not well. I do hope that you will soon be better than I have been. Thanks for the £1. I will drink to your health. By the way I am 87 years of age today. Dear brother let me know a few lines from you, in your next letter, how you are keeping.*
>
> *Phil*[80]

In London, Scottie became friendly with the mother of the English painter Lucian Freud and would borrow small amounts from her as well. Victor Musgrave recalled Scottie asking to borrow five pounds from E. L. T. Mesens, which he received and promptly added to a roll of bills he already had.[81]

Upon his return to Great Britain, Scottie quickly found his way into a gallery setting, showing his work in his native city of Glasgow. In September 1945 he received his first press notice in his homeland for an exhibition not scheduled to be seen until October: "Scotty [sic] Wilson is home to his native Glasgow after a ten years sojourn in Canada. . . . Probably the best term [to describe his pictures] is 'mind pictures,' because they come entirely from his inner thoughts, not from any recognisable models. Glasgow's public will be the first in Europe to see its fellow townsman's strange inspirations. An exhibition of some 350 examples will open for two weeks on October 17 in Messrs. James McLure and Son's picture galleries, Wellington-street."[82]

Additionally, Scottie had his first London exhibition in October 1945. The capital was still recovering from the heavy destruction sustained in World War II, but its cultural life was being revived. His work was shown concurrently with *Surrealist Diversity*, an exhibition that showcased the art of such twentieth-century luminaries as Picasso, Paul Klee, and Joan Miró. Although at the Arcade Gallery, the exhibition was staged under the auspices of the London Gallery, directed by Surrealist artist and poet E. L. T. Mesens.[83] In addition, Scottie's work was shown from December to January at the Barcelona Restaurant in London, a place where Surrealist artists would often meet.

Three Vases, 1955–65 (detail of plate 28)

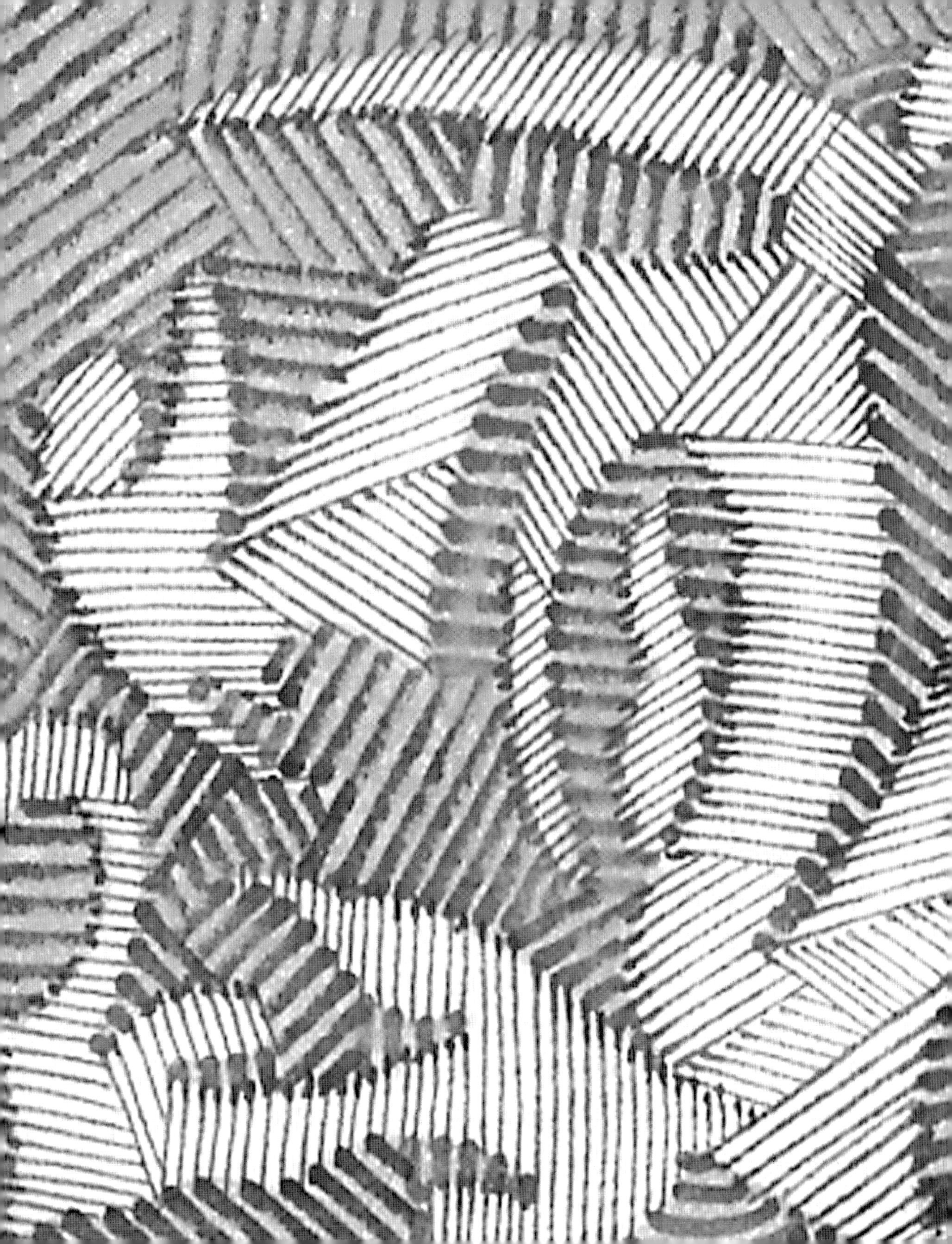

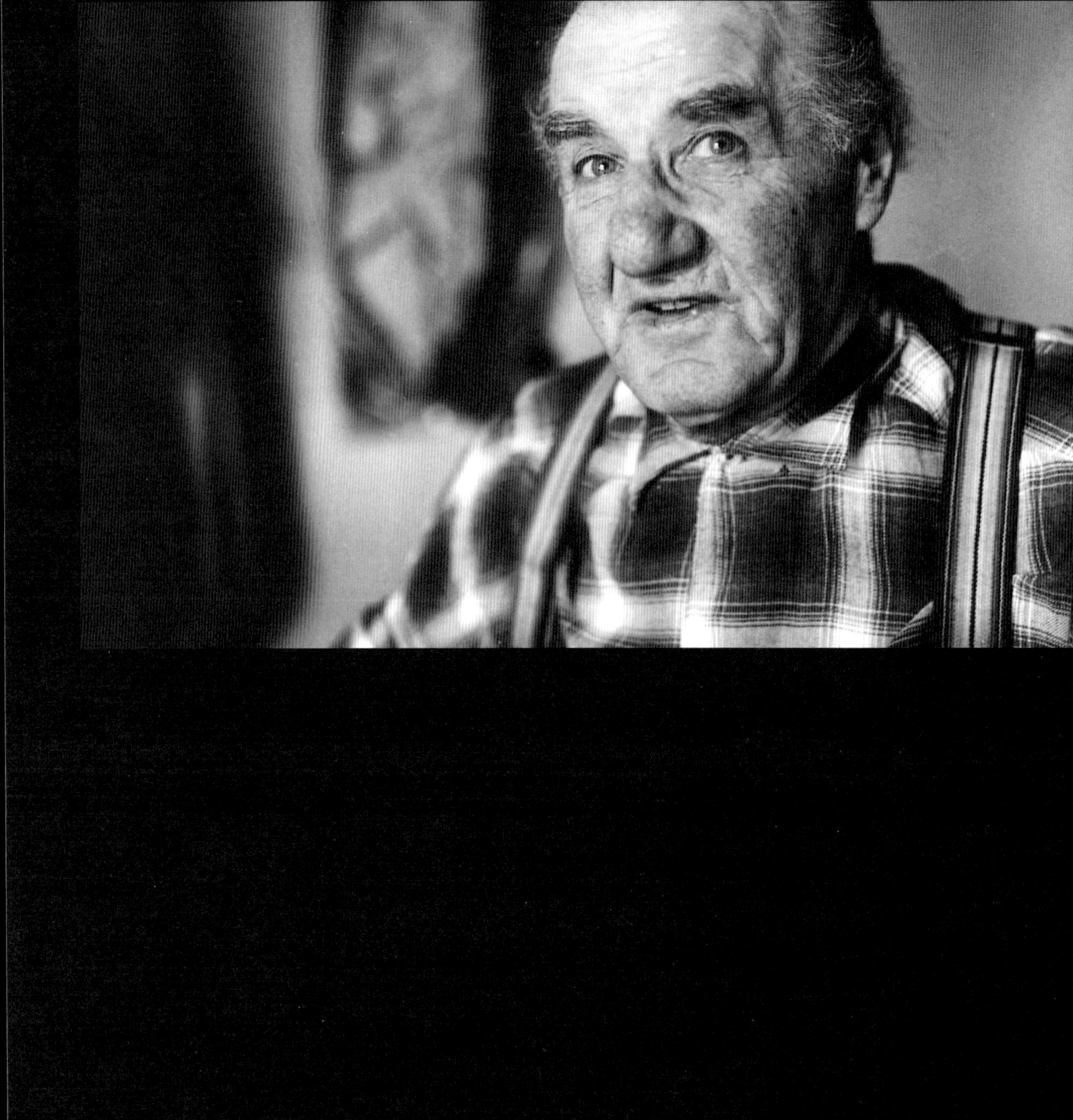

An "Outsider" Artist in London, 1945–72

Because of the dreamlike qualities of his work and his automatist methods, Scottie was categorized as a Surrealist artist, although his intentions were far different from those of the Surrealists and he did not share their intellectual concerns. He had no interest in the artistic output of others, nor was he influenced by external ideas or images. The London art scene and the Surrealists with whom he was suddenly grouped did not hold his attention at all.

Scottie's independence as an artist stood in sharp contrast to the social nature of the Surrealist movement, which was characterized by the sharing of ideas through discussions and collaborative drawings and writings. One of its main objectives was to fuse inner and outer realities, gleaning images directly from the unconscious while rejecting overly analytical or premeditated approaches. The Surrealists used a variety of methods to attempt a connection with pure creativity, and they admired Scottie's work for its facile and sophisticated use of inventive imagery. This method of drawing images from within, from this "interior space," was what he did have in common with the Surrealists.

As Scottie became a recognized sight around leading London galleries, especially Gimpel Fils, which regularly showed his work for a number of years, he infiltrated the cocktail set, but as Roger Cardinal put it, "his attendance was . . . by way of decoration."[84] Various accounts characterize Scottie as a heavy drinker at the time, and he admitted as much to one journalist: "I'm a glutton lad, when they give me liquor. A real glutton."[85] As Scottie advanced in age, he became more reclusive, and his drinking seemed to taper off.

Scottie hovered on the edges of London's art crowd and mounted his own exhibitions, now with a street-savvy scheme of charging admission to see his pictures. A poster promoting an exhibition in Aberdeen, dated November 12, 1945, exhorts the public to see "'Scottie' Wilson, a Glasgow-Born Primitive Artist with his Exhibition

Scottie Wilson, c. 1965–70. Photographer: Ida Kar (1908–74). National Portrait Gallery, London.

of 300 of the most 'Amazing Dream Pictures' Ever Shown to the Public." The adver-
tisement breathlessly describes the exhibition as "the show that startled Canada."

From this poster, a few conclusions can be drawn. First, Scottie put his own name
in quotation marks, emphasizing that it was indeed a nickname, as he had taken
Robert as his new first name. And he referred to himself as a "primitive artist." Not only
is this a sophisticated way for him to describe his work, but it also would have held
a sense of mystery for the viewing public, much like the hyperbolic language of the copy.

It seems that Scottie was becoming aware of his own marketing potential and the
necessity of sales to support himself. A 1949 letter from the Waterman Pen Company
asks for formal written permission for the use of three photographs of his pictures for
advertising and display purposes. In addition to this endorsement, Scottie was adjust-
ing to the practice of parting with his work through gallery sales and his own deals.
But while the price for one of his pictures in the stylish galleries of London could run
upward of one hundred pounds, he would let them go for just a few pounds to the
right person on the street. He never lost his affinity with everyday, working-class people,
as is illustrated by a comment he made to Roger Cardinal in a 1971 conversation.
Scottie spoke of one of his self-promoted exhibitions in the seaside town of Blackpool,
saying of the people who viewed his work in this unpretentious setting, "They're the
intellect you know."[86]

In 1947 Scottie was represented in the *Exposition internationale du surréalisme* at the
Galerie Maeght in Paris, organized by André Breton, a leader of the Surrealist movement.
This and subsequent gallery exhibitions enhanced Scottie's European reputation as
a Surrealist and primitive and eventually as an "outsider" artist. The exhibition was also
Jean Dubuffet's first in-person look at Scottie's work. A well-known painter in his
own right, Dubuffet started collecting the work of self-taught and marginalized artists
about five years before he met Scottie Wilson. Like many other artists, then and now,
he found inventive techniques and a freedom of expression in the works of self-taught
artists. Dubuffet called it "work produced by people immune to artistic culture in
which there is little or no trace of mimicry."[87]

Dubuffet included Scottie's work in the Collection de l'Art Brut, thus acknowledging
him as an Art Brut artist. Literally translated as "raw art," the term Art Brut has
been used since the mid-twentieth century to refer to work made by untutored artists
working outside fine art conventions. Unlike folk art, this work does not carry
on traditional forms, and its creators may not even consider their work to be art. Scholars
of Art Brut, or outsider art—the most commonly used English term, following the
title of Roger Cardinal's 1972 book—are engaged in ongoing discussions about the parame-
ters of this field of work. It is difficult to assign Scottie to any artistic category,
however. He was certainly a visionary, but by his own admission, his drawing was not
a purely automatic process. Although he is frequently considered to be an outsider
artist, he was not culturally isolated, only impervious by his own choice. He was able

Poster promoting a Scottie Wilson exhibition in Aberdeen, Scotland, 1945. Musgrave Kinley Outsider Archive.

to move freely between his humble lodgings and the circles of London gallery life
quite successfully, without compromising his own integrity.

Scottie's choices about what to include or omit from his personal biography
suggest that he was a master marketer. He was constantly changing and shading his life
story to fit whatever the time and circumstances called for. If he thought that he could
influence or persuade a dealer or critic, he would agree with that individual. Curator
Helen Marzolf wrote: "Wilson took perverse delight in more active forms of miscon-
ception. . . . [He] was undoubtedly aware of the marketing potential of a colourful
character."[88]

Ever the independent spirit, Scottie continued to arrange his self-promoted
exhibitions, even while his work was being shown in established galleries. One such
episode was in 1948, when his work was included in an exhibition of automatist art at the
London Gallery. Scottie was concurrently renting "a bombed-out shop in Oxford Street,"
as George Melly described it, where he installed his own show, abiding by his do-it-
yourself ethic. Melly recounts the observations of Victor Musgrave: "Every inch of the
walls were covered by unframed pictures held in place by drawing pins. The effect
was overwhelming. None of the works seemed to be for sale but there was a plate on a table
appealing for a donation of silver. The show was crowded and Scottie moved among
the public talking to them about his pictures and drawing their attention to the press
cuttings which were on display."[89]

For a while Scottie would hang his works in a double-decker bus, which would
travel to various seaside and resort towns, going to Cardiff in the west and to the eastern
shore at Margate.[90] At times he would set up his own exhibitions and charge people
just to view his work, as he had done earlier in Canada.

During the 1950s Scottie's "colourful character" may have helped to secure him
a place in the prismatic London art scene. The focus was indeed on the city; anywhere
else was essentially regarded as a cultural backwater. As noted by curator and author
Martin Harrison, "A definition of British art in the Fifties would need to encompass
at least Neo-Romanticism, Social Realism, Geometric and Painterly Abstraction, and
Pop-Art."[91] In this stew, Scottie continued to draw and make a living from his work,
showing in the city and venturing out into the "hinterlands" for his self-promoted
exhibitions. Although his work continued to be shown in London, he certainly was not
part of the group that flocked to the exhibitions of the American Abstract Expressionists
and their followers.

Bill Hopkins, a London author and critic, first met Scottie in 1950. Hopkins said that
Scottie was in fact suspicious of almost everyone, including art dealers. He never sold
exclusively through one gallery and regularly sold on his own in England and Canada,
even while working with Douglas Duncan. Scottie was no more trusting as a painter
than he was as a peddler. He had been self-sufficient all his life, and being part of the
art world wouldn't change anything. His dislike of authority figures and intellectuals

applied equally to gallery owners, politicians, and anyone else he thought had a superior attitude. In light of his difficult childhood, lack of education, on-again, off-again military career, and the possible influence of the IRA, his attitude is understandable.

Speaking about showing his art in galleries, Scottie told Mervyn Levy that it was "too good for them, too beautiful for this so-called civilization; too truthful for those mouthpieces. You can't talk to intellectuals . . . they can only hear themselves babbling a lot of stupid muck—lot of blah blah. They get paid for it too!"[92]

In London, Scottie's lifestyle was quite modest. He rented an inexpensive single room and spent little money on food and clothing, except for hats from exclusive shops and boots from an expensive boot maker in Saint James. He favored well-made riding boots, always highly polished, which he had cut down at considerable expense. The hats and boots, which stood in marked contrast to the rest of his rather shabby appearance, were the only indulgences he allowed himself after all the years of eking out an existence. He even smoked Woodbines, the workingman's cigarettes.[93]

Only in the military did Scottie have a dependable income. For the rest of his adult life—whether he was a street peddler, a shopkeeper, or an artist—there was no guarantee of any money coming in. So being frugal was practical, but cultivating the appearance of a common man was also good for business. It was what he thought people would expect from a man of his working-class background. And the lifestyle was in keeping with the many stories he told about his humble past. It wouldn't be prudent to look too successful.

So Scottie's lifestyle played a part in his unconventional business model. He did not seem to find himself to be eccentric, only misunderstood. His personal pantheon included William Blake, Robert Burns, and Charlie Chaplin, and he felt that these men were the only people who would have been capable of understanding his work.[94] He also looked forward to discussing his work with the heavenly host: "D'ye think the angels don't know my work? They love it, and when my time comes I'm ready for a good talk with them. I'm looking forward to meeting Willie Blake too."[95]

A brief statement with a cryptic finish offers some clues to his familiarity with Blake. When asked what he thought of becoming a known and established artist, he credited his success to fate and expressed an empathy for great artists, remarking: "Ooh, it's nothing. It was written down for me at the start. My life has always been guided. All I know is it's in me. It's something you can't explain. Those Old Masters, now, if they were here they'd understand what I mean. It's like thousands of people in Paris used to be showing me magazines, and telling me about Blake. But I wasn't surprised. I couldn't explain it, but I could see how he did those things. People have been copying me for the last 7,000 years."[96]

In spite of his deeply held opinions on the state of the world and his readiness to share them, when it came to giving titles to his works, Scottie often went along with whatever suggestions were made by dealers and friends. Thus, one of his late motifs became known as a "tree of life," but it is unclear whether Scottie specifically intended such symbolism.[97]

Scottie the merchant-artist was extroverted when necessary—a free-spirited man
of the world. But privately he was quite different. Bill Hopkins described Scottie as a bit
of a puritan. He never swore or made sexual references. When Hopkins shared a room
with him on a trip to France, Scottie had to turn off all the lights before he would
undress for bed.

Hopkins and Wilson traveled to France at the request of Jean Dubuffet, who had
seen Scottie's work at the 1947 *Exposition internationale du surréalisme* in Paris.
Hopkins recalled:

> *When Wilson received Dubuffet's letter inviting him to Paris and asking him to bring his portfolio,
> he didn't know anything about Dubuffet or* art brut, *but the prospect of selling his drawings
> appealed to him. Since I was a close friend of Scottie, he insisted that I accompany him. Like a cat,
> he was always wary of strangers.*
>
> *When we arrived, not only was Dubuffet waiting, Pablo Picasso was with him. Both owned a few
> of Scottie's pieces, and Picasso had come to see—and perhaps buy—some more. I vividly remember
> both artists eagerly admiring Scottie's work, squabbling in their fierce, theatrical, Gallic voices
> over who would buy which piece. Scottie accepted their homage with a grin but was somewhat matter-
> of-fact, as he would be with any interested buyer. Looking back, I realize that Scottie's reluctant
> excursion to Paris was one of the defining moments in the exploration of outsider art and that Picasso
> played an important role, hitherto unrecorded, as confidant and collaborator in the early
> evolution of this genre.*[98]

It may appear that Scottie took his association with Dubuffet rather lightly. He made
a point of confusing or mispronouncing many well-known names, especially Picasso's,
and he referred to Dubuffet as "that bloke Buffit."[99] Nevertheless, he often carried a note
written by "Buffit" as a way of presenting his credentials and proving himself to be
an artist of importance.

Scottie Wilson was not influenced by Dubuffet, Picasso, or other established artists but
was profoundly affected by nature; birds, fish, and trees are recurring motifs in his work.
(And, incidentally, they are the three major components of the City of Glasgow crest.)
The leering and menacing faces, known as greedies and evils, in his earlier pictures
are often seen as depictions of negative things, while motifs drawn from nature symbolize
purity and goodness.[100] Scottie does not appear to have been religious, but he had
definite moral thoughts on society—"this wicked world," as he often called it.

Although there is an idealistic undertone to his work, Scottie also retained a sense
of humor about it. In his early drawing days, when asked how he made his work,
he quipped with a wink and a grin, "A Chinaman does them for me!" But perhaps
humor was Scottie's way of avoiding something he couldn't explain. He didn't really
know why he drew the way he did, which is true of most outsider artists. And reportedly,
to deflect attention from himself, he sometimes used the "Chinaman" story when
people made fun of or laughed at his drawings. Scottie said: "When I'm working I can

see what's happening, and I can imagine what's going to happen. I can see best when I'm finishing my pictures with a pen. When I'm making strokes, hundreds and thousands of strokes. I can see then very clearly."[101]

Adopting a more cynical approach, especially in his later years, Scottie often felt that he did indeed see the world more clearly and was keenly aware of its harsh injustices. Always distrustful of politicians and bureaucracy, he easily slipped into a heated diatribe. Mervyn Levy recounts Scottie's words: "Civilisation is bloody. The whole atmosphere is awful. This country gets away with murder. The judges, the juries. . . . Oh, I can see this world better than 90 per cent of the people who run it, even today now I'm old. And it's all come true. I can tell out of my own feelings if decisions is right or wrong."[102]

Scottie was often viewed as an eccentric character. Largely illiterate, he dismissed books, saying that he didn't need them because his head was full of books. It was also full of ideas about a mystical sort of universe, a utopian world that could come through his art. The peace and serenity of his paintings from the second half of his artistic career attest to this, but ideas for societal change were already germinating early in his postwar London years. In a 1949 interview he startled and charmed one reporter: "Scottie tells me he is selling off all his present work in order to clear the way for a new conception—'Mars' paintings, which are to be the basis for 'a new civilisation and a new clientele.' His work has a weird fascination and looks charmingly decorative indoors. I know, because I bought three and they are growing on me."[103] Scottie even came up with a rather cryptic name to describe his kind of drawing, calling it Somnarticulism. But it seems that he used this term only briefly, at the end of the 1940s.

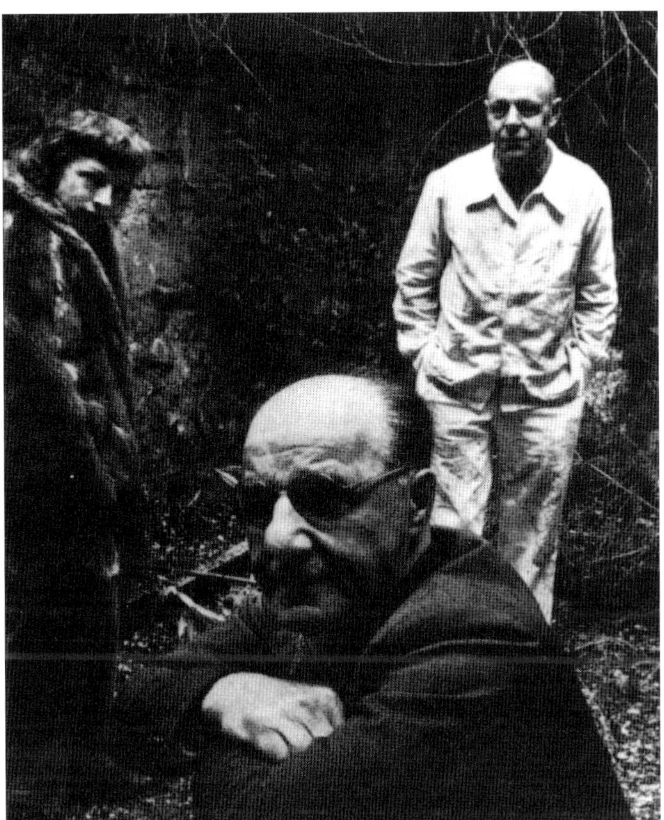

Jean and Lili Dubuffet at their home in rue de Vaugirard with Scottie Wilson, Paris 1950/51.
©Archives Fondation Dubuffet, Paris

As Scottie became entrenched in the London art world, he became more aware of its mechanics but remained completely uninterested in artistic fashion. But he did have his opinions on modern art. In a 1966 article entitled "The Visionary of Kilburn," he commented on seeing some pictures in a London art gallery window before going to Canada. "I remember seeing some pictures in the window. I'd call them 'abstract' today now I'm civilized, but then they seemed to me just stupid, and I said to myself,

'I'd love to do something different.' You see, I've always loved doing masterpieces."[104]

From the middle to late part of his drawing career, Scottie's work changed, not so much in style or subject, but in compositional technique. His pictures retained the distinctive hatching and selectively applied color, but the scenes became more decorative, more serene, and to some eyes, less compelling. The images of malevolent evils and greedies gave way to quiet and peaceful birds, trees, and castles. There is a delicacy in the gentle images, appealing in their own right but lacking the emotional intensity of earlier pieces.

In retrospect, the drawings of Scottie's postwar period, particularly works from the 1950s onward, are quite different from his earlier pieces. Still they received warm reviews in London as well as European countries. Scottie may not have traveled much during this time, but his art did. It was shown in New York, Switzerland, and France. In *Les Lettres françaises*, one reviewer struggled with the question that still plagues viewers today—exactly how does one describe the work of Scottie Wilson? "Is Scottie a primitive? No . . . he is a pure master of astounding technique and of a lasting poetry. His fantasy is perfectly natural; we rarely hear a poet sing so truly."[105]

Scottie's well-cultivated character prompted many colorful descriptions of him and his work. Because of his penchant for storytelling or self-mythologizing, there were some interesting details that were reported, but it seems that they must be taken with a grain of salt. One such story is that his artistic interests were actually sparked during his childhood, when in a tavern he would draw with his fingers on the wet surface of the bar while waiting for his father.[106] Another article described his daily working routine: "Some days he worked over his [drawing] board as many as 15 hours a day, turned out pictures in two days. Afternoons at 4, however, he took time off to have tea with his landlady's cat."[107]

In the 1960s Scottie became interested in painting plates. He picked up some inexpensive dishes from Woolworth's and painted designs on them. Pleased with the results, he told a reporter, "China is what I've always wanted to do."[108] The suitability of Scottie's art for ceramics was noticed as early as 1949 by David Waring, who wrote: "Actually, many of these designs could be successfully applied to objects where form and pattern are closely linked." He cited one drawing in particular that "seem[ed] to cry out for a potter who could realise it in china."[109] After a few experiments, Scottie developed a deft touch for this painting medium, opening up an entirely new path for his work.

In 1962 some of Scottie's plates were exhibited at the Ben Uri Gallery in London, which showed primarily work by Jewish artists.[110] Was Scottie now embracing the heritage that for so long he had seemed to disguise? In 1978 Irving Grosse, director of the Ben Uri Gallery, included Scottie's work in the exhibition *Jewish Artists of Great Britain, 1845–1945*. In the introductory comments in the catalogue, Grosse wrote that while some artists were very proud of their Jewish heritage, others were sensitive and secretive, worried about being stigmatized."' If Scottie was ever terribly concerned about this, his unease seems to have lessened over time. The 1962 exhibition is one of the earliest instances of his work being presented in a distinctly Jewish context.

His painted plates led to other opportunities for Scottie. Through the influence of Professor Robert Baker, then the art director of Royal Worcester Porcelain Company, Scottie was offered a contract to produce a tableware design. Neal French, who at the time was a young designer at the company, wrote an article for *Ceramic Review* in which he shared his first impressions of Scottie: "[Scottie] visited the factory soon after, a small gnomelike, shy and almost unintelligible Glaswegian with an enormous sense of wonder and fun, but no idea at all about fitting designs on to dinnerware. After all, if he wanted a design on a plate he just painted it there."[112]

French was assigned to work with Scottie in adapting his art to the fittings used to design the plates. Scottie had difficulty painting on the cardboard pieces because once he got the paint on them "they reared up 'like snakes' and he was frightened."[113] Eventually his troubles were overcome, but still French had to counsel him against his inclination toward filling the entire surface with decoration. It wasn't practical for the pattern, and it was costly for the company.

French recalled a humorous anecdote that showed Scottie's generosity, fondness for the zoo, and love of sweets, all in the same gesture: "I think it was the next time he came [to the office] he handed out sweets and cakes from a paper bag to all of the designers because, sitting at our desks divided by screens, we reminded him of animals at the zoo." Two patterns were produced—one with black images on a terra-cotta background and the other with black and gray images on a light-colored background. They were not a commercial success, probably because of the price of the pieces, but the designs were widely admired. In fact, the earl of Snowden bought a complete set after seeing them. French remarked that, even though the dishes are still collected today, "[the] pity is that they could not have been on breakfast tables across the country."[114]

Scottie's designs were used not only for dinnerware but also for textiles. He produced two patterns for textile company Edinburgh Weavers, and one of his designs was used for a scarf by the renowned English textile house of Ascher. During the second quarter of the twentieth century, Ascher came up with the idea of commissioning modern artists to create designs for scarves. A number of artists participated, including Henri Matisse and Henry Moore. In the mid-1950s a Scottie Wilson scarf was produced. Only three hundred were manufactured, making it very rare indeed. The scarf was displayed in an exhibition at the Victoria and Albert Museum honoring the creativity and quality of the pieces produced by Ascher.

In yet another creative leap from his drawings, Scottie was commissioned to produce a mural for the headquarters of a Swiss bank. According to Scottie's telling of the story, he was hosted by the bank president in his chalet. He recalls the view from his accommodations: "I could look out to the high mountains on the other side of a lake, and there were wee castles all over them with lights that sparkled like stars at night. It was beautiful. I painted pictures of that."[115] There is an irony, as noted by George Melly, in the selection of Scottie as the artist for this project. Melly recounts Scottie's experience at the luncheon given in his honor to commemorate the completion of the project. Scottie, speaking to London art dealers Rene and Kay Gimpel, said: "There were the bankers with all their bags of gold, and me sitting there without the price of a kipper in me pocket."[116] In his customary way, Scottie was likely exaggerating his financial situation; he was paid three hundred pounds for the commission. In the end, he took a rather prosaic view of the project: "The pubs got the money in the finish, all them lager beer pubs. I enjoyed it. That's your life. I might have come home sooner and been run over by a bus and never done that mural."[117]

The 1960s were a busy time for Scottie. Not only was he continuing to produce art, but he was achieving greater renown. He was even selected as the subject of a television program, but this did not sit well with him. Journalist Doug Marshall wrote about the incident in 1963: "He seems to have a particular hatred for television and recently refused to appear as the subject of a This Is Your Life program." Scottie told Marshall: "You can tell

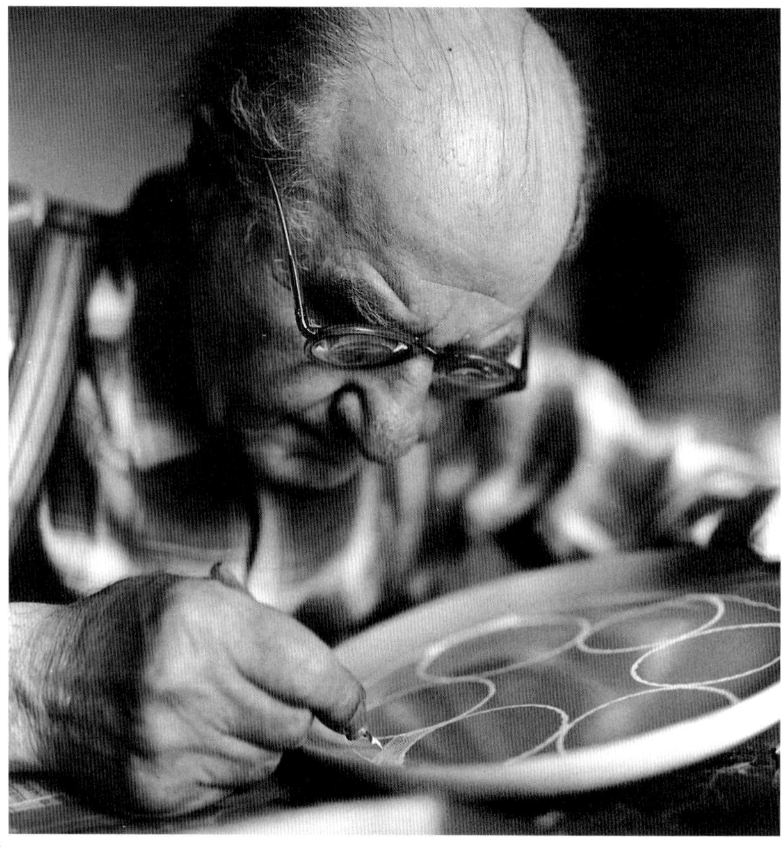

Scottie Wilson, c. 1965–70. Photographer: Ida Kar (1908–74). National Portrait Gallery, London.

them, laddie, that when the world comes to its senses, and people learn the meaning of truth and beauty, then I'll go on television. You can tell them that." Marketing-savvy Scottie followed up this speech with the comment, "That will make a good quote for you." Marshall noted that "there was a twinkle in his eye" as he said it.[118]

Despite "civilization's" continued ignorance of both truth and beauty, Scottie agreed to be filmed by the BBC a scant three years later. A crew visited him in his flat and at the Brook Street Gallery in October of 1966, and he was paid a fee of 78.15 pounds for participating. It is not likely that Scottie had relaxed his critical view of the world, but perhaps he just needed a bit of extra cash.

During the period from the late 1960s to his death in 1972, Scottie's drawings took on a more dramatic quality. Some of these pieces were done on black paper, which set off the bright yellow, white, pink, and green gouache. His motifs remained the same, but instead of using color to fill in the black inked hatch lines, he painted broad marks in color, producing a similar effect with a different technique and medium. A new motif in his work of this time was the butterfly, which appeared alongside his other images. Remarking on the appearance of butterflies in his work, Scottie said: "I've waited 30 years for this. One day I was leaning over this table, trying to think of ideas for new pictures and suddenly it came to me—butterflies . . . there is nothing so real and true as my butterflies."[119]

Although Scottie was advancing in age (having reached his seventy-seventh birthday in 1968), he continued to work. His style changed in favor of thicker paints and wider hatch marks, if any were used at all. He increasingly used broader, bolder areas of flat, bright color. The colors are still quite vivid and striking and may reflect a general vogue for these types of hues during the 1960s.

Scottie wore glasses throughout his life, and in his later works there is a shift away from the detail that characterized his earlier pieces, perhaps due to changes in his eyesight. As early as 1963 Doug Marshall wrote: "He works in the early morning when the light is best for his weakening eyes."[120] In pieces that do show his signature hatching, the lines are widely spaced, evenly positioned, and judiciously used.

Scottie traveled to his exhibitions less and less, citing fatigue as the reason. Mentally he was still sharp and had become more attentive to his own financial situation, which was the subject of rumor and speculation. He still lived modestly, and it was said that he carried his money in suitcases.[121] In contrast to his attitude about selling his pictures some thirty-five years earlier, he had come to grips with the notion of their financial worth and regarded them as a means to security. About his pictures with his favorite new motif, he commented, "I can do enough of these butterfly paintings that will last me—even if I live to be 100."[122] His satisfaction with this new imagery was also reflected in the patient manner in which he completed the pictures. He now understood the ways of the art world, but for him his pictures were all that really mattered. He said: "I can sell them up to £40 and £50 to the dealers, and I know the dealers get a lot more. But I take my time. The longer it takes to produce one of these pictures the more pleased you are."[123]

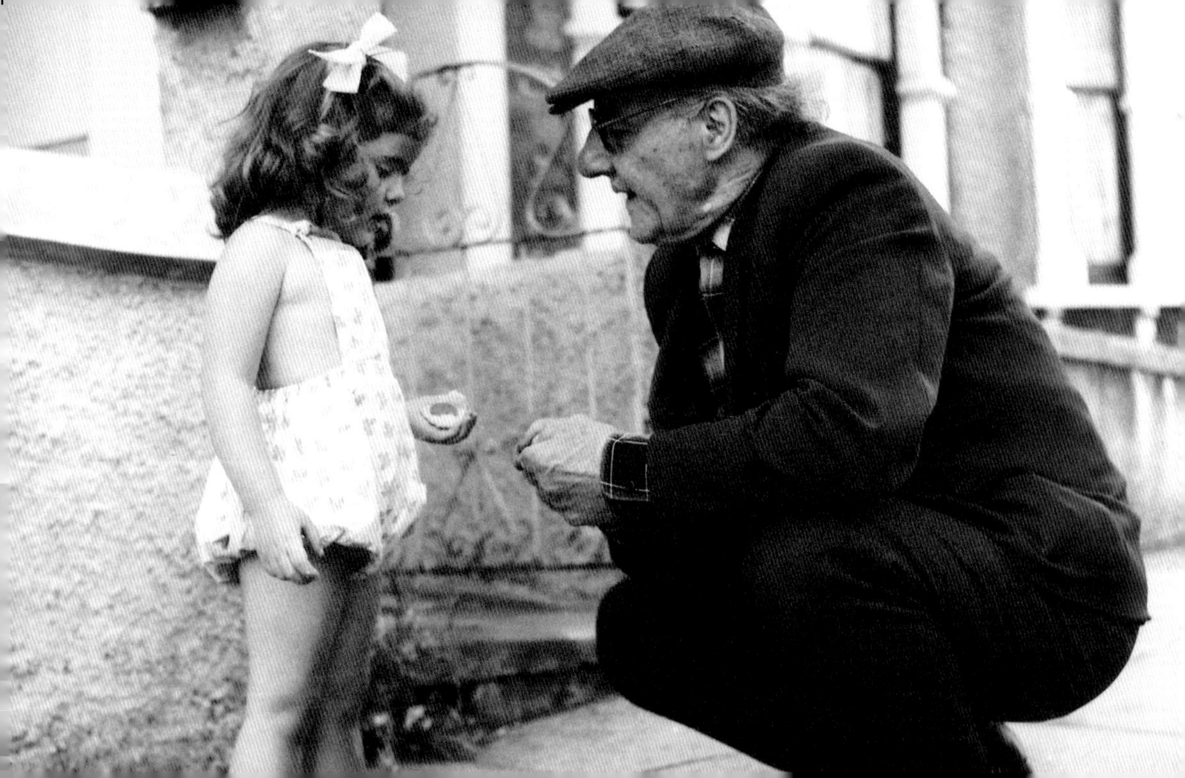

Scottie's Legacy

For the last fourteen years of his life, Scottie lived in a single room of a private home
at 37 Lynton Road, Kilburn, in northwest London. It was the longest he had lived
in a single place as an adult. Journalists and friends—including Mervyn Levy, Victor
Musgrave, and Monika Kinley—visited Scottie in his tiny living room and studio.
It was quite small, just enough for a few sticks of furniture: a bed, wardrobe and cupboard,
a wooden chair, and a table where he created his pictures. It must have been a very
crowded room, for he saved a large number of letters, cards, doctor's appointment
cards, pieces of legal correspondence, gallery announcements, and many newspaper
clippings about him and his art.

Curiously, at the time of his death in 1972 he still had a 1950 national identity
card, a 1953–54 Ministry of Food ration book for Robert Wilson, and radio rental
reminder cards from 1959 to 1963. Presumably, he purchased a radio after that time.
And, as is still the law in the United Kingdom, he had broadcast receiving licenses
from 1958 to 1971. In those days the annual fee was about ten shillings. (Today the
annual fee, which funds the BBC, is 116 pounds [about $192 U.S.] for all the radios
and televisions in a household.)

By this time in his life Scottie was at least able to read headlines and the most
elementary text. He used childish printing when required. And when he needed to save
information, he simply added a calling card, scrap of paper, or envelope to a pile,
which served as his address book. He spoke with friends by telephone and apparently
did little writing when sending gifts. And it is interesting to note that British Telecom
has no record of a Louis Freeman, or Scottie or Robert Wilson, ever having a telephone
listing in London. In all probability, he used the landlord's telephone—completely
in character with his frugal nature.

What is odd about all the items found in his room is that there was nothing
with a date prior to his Toronto Picture Loan Society exhibitions of 1944 and 1945

Scottie Wilson, c. 1965–70. Photographer: Ida Kar (1908–74). National Portrait Gallery, London.

(the 1943 exhibition did not have any announcement) and a formal photo of Scottie
in suit, vest, and tie, taken in May 1943. It's as if his life started when he had his first
exhibition, at age fifty-two. He saved nothing else dated before that time. The only
correspondence he seems to have had with any member of his large family was the
single letter from his brother Philip.

To the end Scottie maintained an independent lifestyle, doing his own laundry and
cooking on a little hotplate in his room. He was seen around the neighborhood as he
did his grocery shopping or went out
for an afternoon coffee at a local café.
One reviewer commented: "He goes
out to shop and feed the sparrows."[124]
Scottie kept to a routine schedule,
according to Mervyn Levy: "Scottie's
working day is very simple. Usually
the artist gets up at six, though
sometimes as early as four. He potters
around and thinks until the eight
o'clock news, after which he returns
to bed again for an hour. From
nine until twelve-thirty he works.
Then he shops, lunches, sleeps in the
afternoon, works in the evening,
and gets to bed somewhere between
midnight and 1 a.m. He cooks for
himself, taking all his meals at home,
his basic diet consisting of eggs,
cheese, kippers and chicken."[125]

Although Scottie was more
reclusive in his later years, he
frequently sent out little gifts of

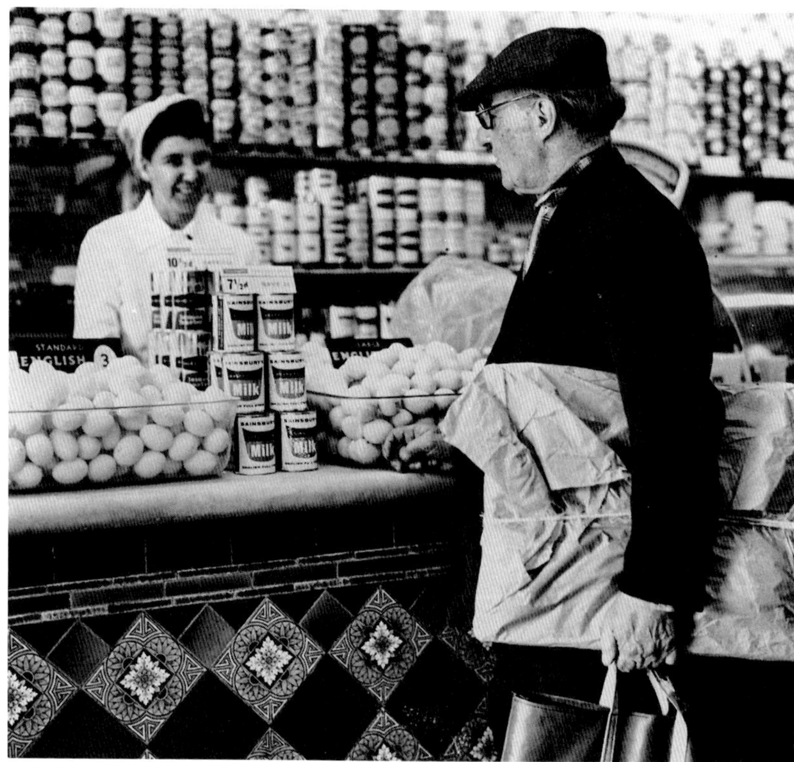

Scottie Wilson, c. 1965–70. Photographer: Ida Kar (1908–74). National Portrait Gallery, London.

candy or fruits to friends and people he was fond of, including Marie-Bernard and the
other sisters at Saint Joseph's Hospital, where he was once a patient. A few very special
people would be honored with one of his drawings. Late in his life he gave friends the
seven-by-six-inch lone butterfly gouache paintings.

On November 23, 1971, Scottie received a letter from an official at Inland Revenue,
requesting that he come in for "A short discussion of your Income Tax Liability."
The dreaded taxman had caught up with Scottie Wilson. After the initial meeting,
the official was now referring to tax liability for past years, and advised, "I should like
you to consider putting the matter into the hands of an accountant or other profes-
sional advisor." It was later learned that the tax inspector had made inquiries regarding

Scottie's financial situation with his friend Dr. Myerson, who was not of much help. The issue was not resolved during Scottie's lifetime.[126]

The peddler turned painter died of cancer on March 26, 1972.[127] He was cremated at Golders Green in London. About twenty friends were in attendance, including Mervyn and Marie Levy; Barry Fealdman, secretary of the Ben Uri Gallery; and a representative of UNICEF.[128]

Alan Rubenstein, a solicitor and cousin of Mervyn Levy, had been handling Scottie's affairs since at least 1967 and took care of many issues regarding his estate. Like many who knew him, he was an admirer of Scottie's artwork. In a March 3, 1967, letter to Scottie he wrote, "As you have asked for a bill I enclose same herewith but I can assure you that my secretary and I would be much happier with a sample of your wonderful work, even though the value of my services may not yet equal one of your plates."[129]

Just after Scottie's death, Rubenstein called Mr. and Mrs. Czyzynski, the owners of house at 37 Lynton Road. He informed them that he was the executor of Scottie's estate and would come by to collect his belongings. In addition to all the artwork, art supplies, clothes, and papers, Rubenstein found a suitcase full of money and records of bank accounts under Scottie's bed. The exact amount is not known, but one relative estimated the cash at five hundred pounds and the bank accounts at seven thousand pounds.[130] This was quite a surprise to all who believed that he was simply an impoverished artist.

Robert "Scottie" Wilson—eccentric loner, lifetime peddler, accomplished artist, and master of deception—had accumulated a considerable sum of money. But it is doubtful that the money meant much to him, except for providing security. More likely, it was a symbol of his artistic accomplishment and a statement to the world that, despite his humble background, he had earned the respect of friends, patrons, and the art community. He was quite pleased with his success. Finding his talent and passion for art was a stroke of luck that made him a very contented man.

Scottie Wilson was eulogized in many newspapers in the United Kingdom, Canada, the United States, and Europe. An obituary in the *Toronto Daily Star* remembered him as a humble artist: "Wilson's work hangs in the Tate and in the leading galleries of Paris and New York but he did not push for fame or fortune. He was content with his shabby bedroom, littered with inks, pens, crayons, old clothes and fruit and his great joy was to shuffle down the street, giving candy to children."[131]

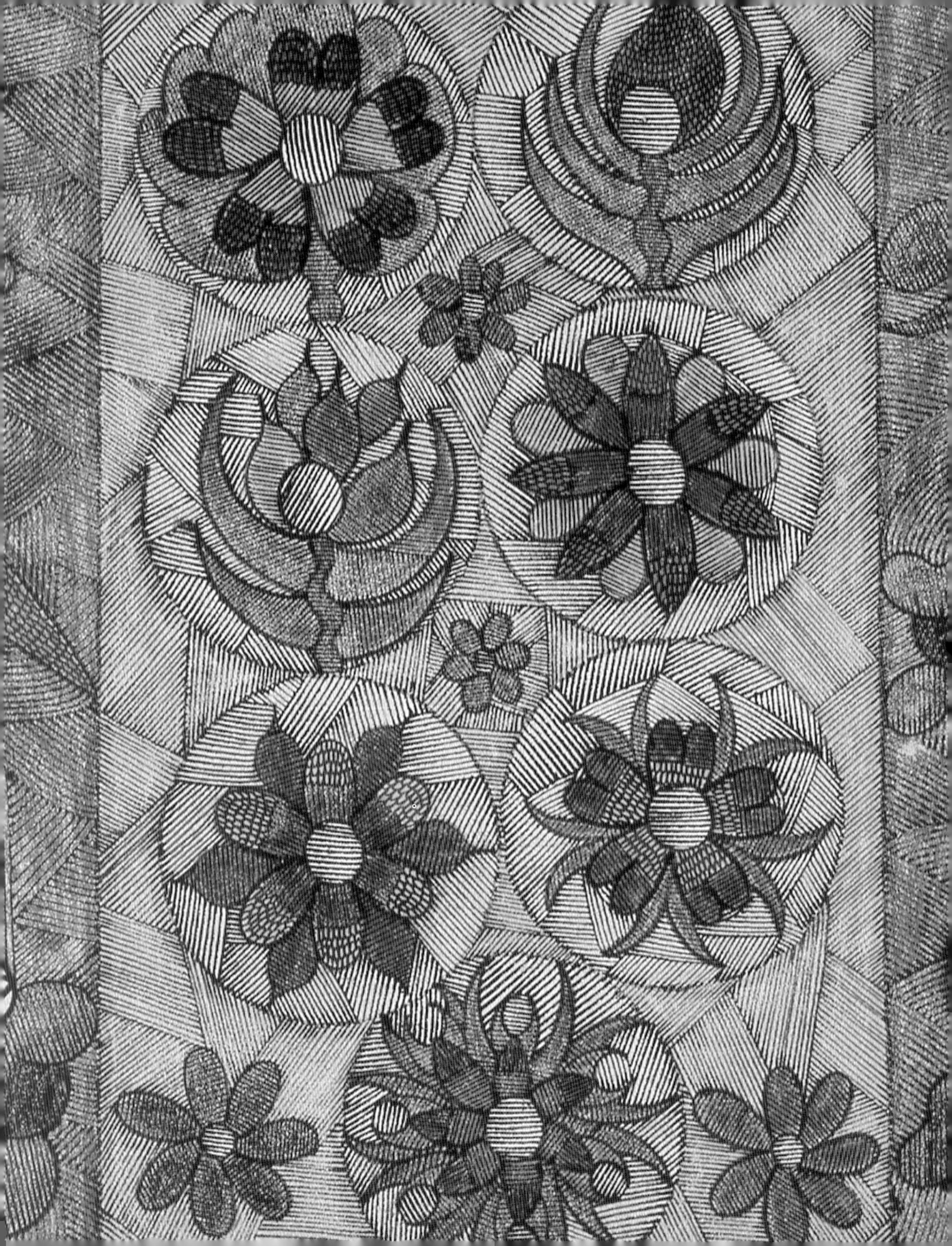

Notes

1. Stuart Underhill, "Career in Art Started in Table-Top Drawing," *Halifax Chronicle Herald*, October 19, 1949. In this account, however, Underhill writes that Scottie left for Canada in 1938, not 1932, as other evidence suggests.

2. Scottie Wilson most often described himself as having three brothers: Philip, Jack, and Frank. The name Philip is clearly indicated in census records, but the identities of the other two, Jack and Frank, are less certain. There are several references to Jack in existing correspondence and publications, and it is possible that the brother named Lazarus assumed the nickname Jack. Great-grandchildren of Julius and Esther report that there were three more children after Louis, two boys and one girl, whose names have been cited as David, Charlie, and Bess.

3. Various sources have listed Julius and Esther as being born in Finland (according to the 1891 Scotland census), Russia, and Lithuania.

4. Alan Freeman to Victor Musgrave, April 7, 1984, Musgrave Kinley Outsider Archive, London. George Melly also cites this source, adding that the couple disembarked at Hull, England (*It's All Writ Out for You: The Life and Work of Scottie Wilson* [London: Thames and Hudson, 1986], 18). The 1891 census records show that the eldest child in the Freeman family, aged twelve, was born in England, suggesting that the Freemans immigrated no later than 1879.

5. A number of factors prompted this increase in emigration, but this subject is beyond the scope of this book. For information pertaining specifically to Jewish immigration to Great Britain, see Kenneth E. Collins, ed., *Aspects of Scottish Jewry* (Glasgow: Glasgow Jewish Representative Council, 1987), and Lloyd P. Gartner, *The Jewish Immigrant in England, 1870–1914*, 3rd ed. (London and Portland, Ore.: Vallentine Mitchell, 2001).

6. See Collins, *Aspects of Scottish Jewry*, 8.

7. On a few occasions Scottie mentioned a brother named Jack, with whom he sold patent medicines on the street. There is no mention of Jack in the historical and legal records, but a letter from the wife of a great-nephew, recounting some of the family history, notes a brother Jack who "sold 'medices' out in the sticks wearing a white coat and monacle [*sic*]. He did not say he was a Doctor but he did not deny it" (Evelyn Mitchell to George Melly, March 21, 1986, Musgrave Kinley Outsider Archive).

8. "The Other Wilson," *Observer Review*, February 9, 1969.

Square with Seven Circles, 1950 (detail of plate 12)

9. Doug Marshall, "Former Toronto Junk Man Wins International Fame," *Ottawa Journal*, May 2, 1963.

10. Mamie Crichton, "Scottie Wilson," *Scottish Field*, July 1974, 36–37.

11. Information on the Scottish Rifles provided by Bill Tilley, Livingston, Scotland, historian for the first battalion Cameronians (correspondence with authors, conducted May–July 2003).

12. Letter from Linda and Jack Forbes to George Melly, June 30, 1986, Musgrave Kinley Outsider Archive. Linda Forbes relayed this information told to her by her father-in-law, Morris Forbes (Goldfarb), a son of Sarah (neé Freeman) and nephew of Scottie Wilson.

13. Some soldiers of Jewish descent objected to being allied with Russia on account of the history of persecution and anti-Semitic governmental policies, but there were many others who enlisted nonetheless. See Collins, *Aspects of Scottish Jewry*, 23.

14. Correspondence in the Musgrave Kinley Outsider Archive documents author George Melly's attempts to retrieve Scottie's military records for his 1986 monograph (*It's All Writ Out for You*). Due to the paucity of known personal details about Scottie and facts needed to authorize the release of the information, these records appear to be unobtainable.

15. Edwin Mullins, "The Visionary of Kilburn," *Weekend Telegraph*, October 10, 1966.

16. Melly, *It's All Writ Out for You*, 18.

17. Mervyn Levy, *Scottie Wilson* (London: Brook Street Gallery, 1966), 8.

18. Sources citing Wilson's involvement in the Black and Tans include Alasdair Gray, "On the Edge of the Art World," *Times Literary Supplement*, March 14, 1986; Helen Marzolf, *Scottie Wilson: The Canadian Drawings* (Regina, Saskatchewan: Dunlop Art Gallery, 1989); Melly, *It's All Writ Out for You*.

19. For historical value of currency, see John J. McCusker, "Comparing the Purchasing Power of Money in Great Britain from 1264 to Any Other Year Including the Present," Economic History Services, 2001, http://www.eh.net/hmit/ppowerbp/ (accessed July 8, 2003). Conversion calculations via http://finance.yahoo.com/m5?a=11.96&s=GBP&t=USD&c=0 (accessed July 8, 2003).

20. John Keegan, *Winston Churchill* (New York: Viking, 2002), 97–99.

21. Alan Freeman to Victor Musgrave, April 7, 1984, Musgrave Kinley Outsider Archive.

22. There is one mention of Scottie lumberjacking to make a living; see Eric Lister, "Scottie Wilson," in *British Primitive Fantasists: A Survey of Portal Painters* (New York: Alpine Fine Arts Collection, 1982). It is unclear where this information comes from, and nothing has surfaced to corroborate this account.

23. See Christopher Hume, "'Wandering Junk Dealer' Back in Metro," *Sunday Star* (Toronto), May 2, 1982.

24. For more on peddlers and the Jewish community, see Gartner, *Jewish Immigrant*, 57–62.

25. One such source is "Scottie Wilson Worthy of Interest," *Toronto Star*, May 31, 1982. The article states that Wilson "returned to Canada (he had visited here briefly in the 1920s) in 1930 or 1931, and wandered throughout the country from Toronto to Vancouver."

26. Immigration records (1925–35), National Archives of Canada (accessed April 15, 2003).

27. Louis Freeman resided at 889 Dundas Street West. This information comes from the City of Toronto directories, which catalog residents and businesses by name as well as individual addresses.

28. Prior to 1934 this address was occupied by Samuel Richman, who used the property for his shoe repair business, and Anthony Wilkitiz. In 1934 Louis Freeman took Wilkitiz's place, but it is indicated that this was his home address, not his shop. Richman and Freeman shared this address until 1937, when Louis Freeman disappeared from the "name" directory, although he was still listed at this address in the "street" directory. His place was taken by Benjamin Shapiro, another boarder, and presumably a fellow Jew, as were the other occupants of the building.

29. Crichton, "Scottie Wilson," 37.

30. Hume, "Wandering Junk Dealer."

31. Levy, *Scottie Wilson*, 9.

32. Marshall, "Former Toronto Junk Man."

33. "Picture Paid for Meals: Now Glasgow Man Holds Exhibition," *Evening Citizen*, October 6, 1948.

34. Paul Duval, "Scottie Is Puzzled Himself by His 'Dreamt-Up' Pictures," *Telegram*, February 8, 1958.

35. "Automatic Painter's Fear," *News Review*, February 26, 1948.

36. "Scotty [*sic*] Paints Pictures 'From the Hear-r-rt,'" *Vancouver News Herald*, June 24, 1943.

37. These ducks are described as such in Melly, *It's All Writ Out for You*, pl. 36. The appellation is previously noted in "Scottie Wilson," *Publications de la Compagnie de l'Art Brut*, fasc. 4 (1965): 5–31.

38. "Scottie Wilson," *Publications de la Compagnie de l'Art Brut*, 22.

39. Victor Musgrave, "Erotic Cosmos," *Art and Artists* 9 (October 1974): 6–9.

40. Crichton, "Scottie Wilson," 37.

41. "One Man Art Show," *St. Catharines Standard*, June 3, 1944.

42. Victor Musgrave, Essay in *Outsiders* (London: Hayward Gallery, Arts Council of Great Britain, 1979).

43. Brian Volke, review of Dunlop Art Gallery show, *Leader-Post* (Regina, Saskatchewan), May 25, 1989. See also Marshall, "Former Toronto Junk Man" exhibition review in *Toronto Globe and Mail*, February 26, 1944: "Conceiving a quite complicated design in his mind, he blocks out his main color portions with all-over crayon coloring, then works over this greasy surface with pen and ink."

44. "Scotty Paints Pictures," 3.

45. Mullins, "Visionary of Kilburn."

46. Musgrave, "Erotic Cosmos," 7.

47. Victor Musgrave, taped interview with Scottie Wilson, 1964; notes provided by Roger Cardinal, December 20, 2002.

48. E. L. T. Mesens, "'Scottie' Wilson," *Horizon* 13 (June 1946): 402.

49. *Edmonton Museum of Art Bulletin* (April 1956); see also "Pen Pictures: New Style," *St. Ives Times*, January 14, 1955.

50. If we look at the timeline from this period, and with the evidence that Scottie was in Toronto in 1935, we can place him in Vancouver at least in 1938 but possibly earlier. This is corroborated by a letter from Ronald Hambleton to the editor of the *Toronto Star*, dated May 17, 1982, in response to an article by Christopher Hume ("Wandering Junk Dealer"). Hambleton stated that "it was his impression that Wilson lived in Vancouver for a somewhat longer period prior to 1938 but he did not know the dates." Scottie, according to art dealer Douglas Duncan, visited other Canadian cities, but it is not clear if these were merely trips that he took or if he had an extended stay. In 1941–42 he visited Montreal, and in 1942 he was in Winnipeg, where he contacted a representative of the Federation of Canadian Artists, who referred him to H. Garnard (Rik) Kettle. With an introduction from Kettle, Scottie met Douglas Duncan in 1942. This sequence of events brings him back to Toronto and marks the beginning of his career under the mentorship of Duncan.

51. Marzolf, *Scottie Wilson*, 8.

52. An official of the Ontario Ministry of Consumer and Business Services reported that at the time it would have been relatively easy for Scottie to change his name. He could have gone through the court system, but a few well-placed dollars would have accomplished the same

result. Or Scottie could just have assumed his new name and carried on. The official also said that at that time movement between Canada and Britain would have been very easy (telephone interview, May 28, 2003).

53. See Valerie Knowles, "Immigration Slump," in *Forging Our Legacy: Canadian Citizenship and Immigration, 1900–1977* (Ottawa: Citizenship and Immigration Canada, 2000), 43–62.

54. Myer Siemiatycki, "Immigration and Urban Politics in Toronto," paper presented at the Third International Metropolis Conference, Israel, November 29–December 3, 1998, http://www.international.metropolis.net/events/Israel/papers/Siemiatycki.html (accessed July 8, 2003).

55. Gerald Tulchinsky, "Ben Lappin's Reflections on May Day Celebrations in Toronto's Jewish Quarter," *Labour/Le Travail* 49 (2002): 211–21.

56. Melly, *It's All Writ Out for You*, 16.

57. Scottie's activities in Vancouver are not well documented, but he did continue to draw. It is unclear exactly when he arrived there, but it was at least by 1938, according to Ronald Hambleton's account (letter to the editor, *Toronto Star*, May 17, 1982).

58. For more information about Vancouver and the history of its Chinese quarter, see Patricia E. Roy, *The History of Canadian Cities: Vancouver: An Illustrated History* (Toronto: James Lorimer and Company, National Museum of Man, and National Museums of Canada, 1980).

59. Stuart Underhill, "Noted in Britain as Unique Artist, Began in Toronto" (Ontario, 1949). This article was reprinted in various forms in several newspapers. Underhill dates Scottie's return to Vancouver to 1942, however, which we feel is erroneous.

60. Stanley Park is situated on a peninsula and covers more than one thousand acres, making it the largest urban park in North America. It was officially opened in 1888 and was a well-established part of the city by the time of Scottie's arrival in the late 1930s.

61. For more information on the Stanley Park totem poles, see Hilary Stewart, *Looking at Totem Poles* (Vancouver and Toronto: University of Washington Press, 1993), 81–90.

62. Mervyn Levy, "The Artist at Work: Scottie Wilson's Kingdom in Kilburn," *Studio* 163 (June 1962): 226–31.

63. The early years of the 1940s mark a period when Scottie traveled frequently. In 1941 he was in Toronto and Montreal, then was in Winnipeg the following year, according to Marzolf, *Scottie Wilson*, 33. Some newspaper articles indicate that Scottie participated in the 1941 Canadian Exhibition in Toronto, but the exhibition catalogues in the Art Gallery of Ontario archives reveal that he was not among the artists in the show.

64. Hambleton, letter to the editor.

65. "Picture Paid for Meals."

66. "Somnarticulism," *Evening Standard*, October 4, 1948.

67. Alan Jarvis, ed., *Douglas Duncan: A Memorial Portrait* (Toronto and Buffalo: University of Toronto Press, 1974).

68. Crichton, "Scottie Wilson," 37.

69. The exhibition was held from April 17 to April 30, 1943.

70. Pearl McCarthy, review in "Art and Artists" section, *Globe and Mail*, April 17, 1943.

71. Publicity sheet for *Drawings by "Scottie" Wilson*, exhibition assembled for the Western Canada Art Circuit by Douglas Duncan, Toronto, and shown at the Fine Arts Gallery, University of British Columbia, November 3–21, 1953.

72. "Original Exhibition," *Vancouver Province*, June 30, 1943.

73. "Scotty Paints Pictures," 3.

74. "One Man Art Show."

75. This figure is estimated by curator Helen Marzolf (*Scottie Wilson*, 14). More than 125 images are recorded in the Scottie Wilson Inventory, Douglas Duncan and Frances Barwick Fonds, National Gallery of Canada Archives.

76. Numerous sources comment on Scottie's illiteracy, but to what degree he could not read is not fully addressed. The language of this letter does not imply that it was written for someone who had difficulty reading. This suggests that either Scottie's reading skills were not as poor as generally assumed or that he often had people he could rely on to read his correspondence to him.

77. Douglas Duncan to Scottie Wilson, May 23, 1945, Scottie Wilson Archive, Scottish National Gallery of Modern Art, Edinburgh.

78. Alan Freeman to Victor Musgrave, April 7, 1984, Scottie Wilson Archive, Scottish National Gallery of Modern Art, Edinburgh.

79. Linda and Jack Forbes (son of Morris and grandson of Sarah Freeman) to George Melly, June 30, 1986, Musgrave Kinley Outsider Archive, London.

80. Phil Freeman to Scottie Wilson, April 12 (year unknown), Scottie Wilson Archive, Scottish National Gallery of Modern Art, Edinburgh. Freeman does not address Scottie by name in the salutation but instead addresses him as "dear brother."

81. Musgrave, "Erotic Cosmos," 8.

82. Ian More, "Scotland as I See It: Indian Totem Pole Inspired Picture," *Reynolds News and Sunday Citizen*, September 23, 1945.

83. It is uncertain how Scottie Wilson met E. L. T. Mesens or how his premier London show came about. The exhibition was accompanied by a catalogue, according to George Melly, *Don't Tell Sybil: An Intimate Memoir of E. L. T. Mesens* (London: Heinemann, 1997), 116–17. For further information on the Surrealist movement, see: Michel Remy, *Surrealism in Britain* (Aldershot, England, and Brookfield, Vt.: Ashgate, 1999), 316–21.

84. Roger Cardinal, *Outsider Art* (London: Studio Vista, 1972), 79.

85. Marshall, "Former Toronto Junk Man."

86. This anecdote comes from the notes of Roger Cardinal, recording a conversation with Wilson on July 1, 1971. The exchange is also recorded in Cardinal, *Outsider Art*, 79.

87. For further background on Art Brut, see *Publications de la Compagnie de l'Art Brut*, fascs. 1–8 (1964–66); Cardinal, *Outsider Art*; Colin Rhodes, *Outsider Art: Spontaneous Alternatives* (London: Thames and Hudson, 2000); and Lucienne Peiry, *Art Brut: The Origins of Outsider Art* (Paris: Flammarion, 2001).

88. Marzolf, *Scottie Wilson*, 26.

89. Melly, *It's All Writ Out for You*, 41.

90. It is unclear how or when Scottie obtained this bus, but the events are corroborated by his friend George Murray (interviews with the authors, December 2003).

91. Martin Harrison, *Transition: The London Art Scene in the Fifties* (London: Merrell, in association with Barbican Art, 2002), 16.

92. Levy, *Scottie Wilson*, 12.

93. Mervyn Levy, a close friend of Scottie Wilson in the later years of his life, provides many personal details in his book *Scottie Wilson*.

94. Scottie's references to Blake, Burns, and Chaplin are recorded in Musgrave, "Erotic Cosmos," 8, and elaborated upon in Melly, *It's All Writ Out for You*, 53.

95. Melly, *It's All Writ Out for You*, 53.

96. Mullins, "Visionary of Kilburn".

97. As early as 1955, *Tree of Life* was noted as a title of a Scottie Wilson piece; see "Pen Pictures—New Style," *St. Ives Times*, January 14, 1955. In 1966 Mervyn Levy identified *The Tender Tree, Peaceful Village*, and *The Tree of Life* as characteristic titles (*Scottie Wilson*, 4). That year Edwin Mullins described some of Scottie's paintings as "dominated by the Tree of Life" ("Visionary of Kilburn"). In his 1979 book Gérard A. Schreiner lists three different paintings, each titled *Tree of Life* (*Scottie Wilson* [Rorschach, Switzerland: Zehnder, 1979], 5, 19, 47).

98. Anthony Petullo, *Self-Taught and Outsider Art: The Anthony Petullo Collection* (Urbana: University of Illinois Press, 2001), 183.

99. Mullins, "Visionary of Kilburn".

100. Ibid. In this interview with the artist, Mullins notes Scottie's use of the term "greedies" to describe the menacing human figures.

101. Levy, "Artist at Work," 228.

102. Mullins, "Visionary of Kilburn"; Levy, "Artist at Work," 228. Melly provides a concise discussion of Scottie's worldview (*It's All Writ Out for You*, 55–56).

103. "Art Mart," *New Cavalcade*, July 23, 1949.

104. Mullins, "Visionary of Kilburn".

105. Review in *Les Lettres françaises*, February 25, 1953.

106. Review in *Calgary Herald*, January 2, 1954.

107. "Scottie's World," *Time*, September 19, 1949.

108. Marshall, "Former Toronto Junk Man."

109. David Waring, "Scottie Wilson, L. Petley-Jones, Suzanne Freemont: Gimpel Fils Gallery," *Art News and Review*, September 24, 1949.

110. The Ben Uri Art Society was established in 1915 with the goal of supporting and promoting Jewish art in the London community. In 1995 the gallery was awarded museum status.

111. Irving Grosse, *Jewish Artists of Great Britain, 1845–1945* (London: Ben Uri Gallery, 1978).

112. Neal French, "Scottie Wilson," *Ceramic Review*, no. 98 (March–April 1986): 25.

113. Ibid., 25.

114. Ibid., 25, 26.

115. Crichton, "Scottie Wilson," 37.

116. Melly, *It's All Writ Out for You*, 75.

117. "Primitive," *Sunday Times*, March 21, 1965.

118. Marshall, "Former Toronto Junk Man."

119. "Primitive Artist Shuns the Public," *New York Times*, April 2, 1968.

120. Marshall, "Former Toronto Junk Man." Scottie's deteriorating vision in his later years was also noted by Mamie Crichton ("Scottie Wilson," 37): "His spectacles pushed back over his head, brush and plate close up to his weak eyes."

121. "The Mysterious World of Scottie Wilson," *Ottawa Citizen*, March 2, 1968. Also "Primitive Artist Shuns the Public." Telephone interviews conducted in December 2003 with Scottie Wilson's friend George Murray corroborate these accounts.

122. "The Mysterious World of Scottie Wilson," *Ottawa Citizen*, March 2, 1968.

123. "Primitive Artist Shuns the Public."

124. "The Other Wilson," *Observer Review*, February 9, 1949.

125. Levy, "Artist at Work," 229.

126. HM Inspector of Taxes to Scottie Wilson, November 23, 1971, and December 23, 1971, Scottie Wilson Archive, Scottish National Gallery of Modern Art, Edinburgh.

127. According to his death certificate, Scottie Wilson died in his home at 37 Lynton Road, Kilburn, on March 26, 1972. The cause of death, as indicated by Dr. C. T. Myerson, was carcinoma of the bowel. Alan Rubenstein is listed as the informant who provided this information to the General Register Office on March 27, 1972.

128. The United Nations Children's Fund (UNICEF) selected one of his pictures, *Bird Song*, to be included on its annual assortment of Christmas cards in 1970.

129. Alan G. Rubenstein to Scottie Wilson, March 3, 1967, Scottie Wilson Archive, Scottish National Gallery of Modern Art, Edinburgh.

130. One bank account was most likely at Midland Bank Limited, which corresponded with Scottie about his account in February 1969.

131. "Scottie Wilson, 82, Primitive Artist," *Toronto Daily Star*, March 28, 1972.

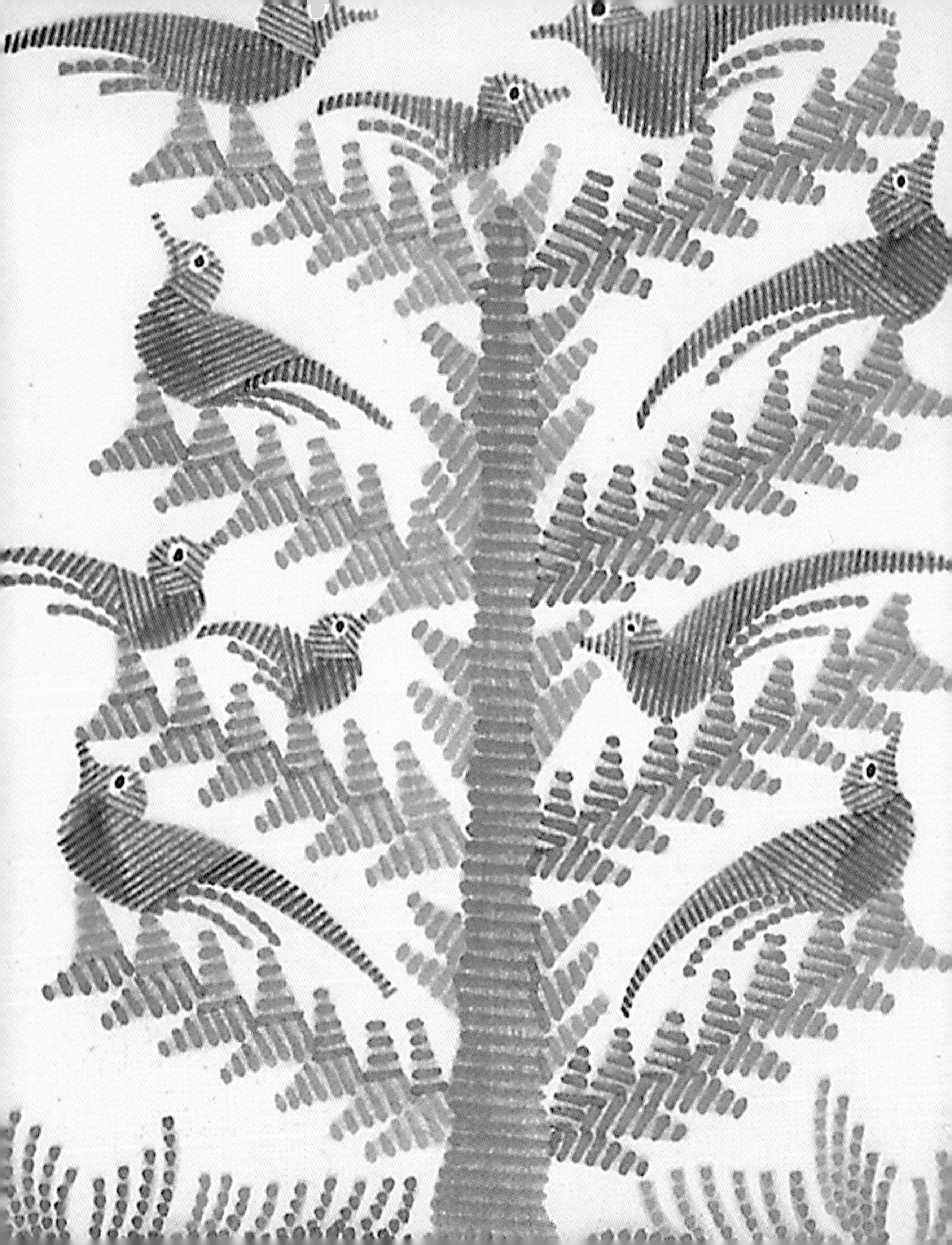

Chronology

<table>
<tr><td>1878</td><td>Julius and Esther Freeman are married in Riga, Latvia.</td></tr>
<tr><td>c. 1880</td><td>Julius and Esther Freeman immigrate to England.</td></tr>
<tr><td>1891</td><td>Louis Freeman is born in Glasgow, Scotland, on February 28.</td></tr>
<tr><td>1906</td><td>Freeman joins the military, serving in the Scottish Rifles.</td></tr>
<tr><td>1911</td><td>At Bloemfontein, South Africa, Freeman buys himself out of the army and works his way back home as a ship's stoker.</td></tr>
<tr><td>1914</td><td>Freeman reenlists to fight in World War I and is stationed in France on the Western Front.</td></tr>
<tr><td>c. 1918–22</td><td>Returning home to a depressed economy and with little hope of finding work, Freeman signs up with the Royal Irish Constabulary, known as the Black and Tans, but deserts to Canada.</td></tr>
<tr><td>1920s</td><td>Returns home after a short stay in Canada; works as a peddler and street trader in Glasgow and London.</td></tr>
<tr><td>c. 1932</td><td>Freeman returns to Canada, eventually settling in Toronto as a peddler.</td></tr>
<tr><td>c. 1935</td><td>In the back of his secondhand shop, Freeman begins drawing on a tabletop; drawing eventually becomes his all-consuming activity.</td></tr>
<tr><td>1938</td><td>Freeman (now also known as Scottie Wilson) leaves Toronto for Vancouver, where he continues his trading business and drawing.</td></tr>
</table>

Red Vase, c. 1960 (detail of plate 26)

1942   Scottie Wilson travels to Winnipeg and contacts a representative of the Federation of Canadian Artists, whose referral eventually leads to his association with Douglas Duncan and the Picture Loan Society.

1943   Scottie's work is shown at the Picture Loan Society, Toronto.

1945   After more exhibitions in Canada (self-promoted as well as gallery shows), Scottie suddenly returns to Scotland and subsequently settles in London, where he is loosely associated with Surrealist art circles.

1947   Scottie's work is included in the *Exposition internationale du surréalisme* in Paris, where it is seen by artist Jean Dubuffet, a leading proponent of Art Brut, or outsider art.

1950   Accompanied by Bill Hopkins, Scottie Wilson travels to Paris at the request of Dubuffet. Wilson and Dubuffet meet for the first time; Wilson and Hopkins also meet Pablo Picasso.

1954   Ascher Textiles includes a Scottie Wilson design as part of its series of scarves featuring the work of modern artists.

1962   Scottie's painted plates are shown at Ben Uri Gallery, London, which leads to a commission from Royal Worcester to design two sets of tableware.

c. 1965   Scottie is commissioned to paint a mural at the headquarters of a bank in Basel, Switzerland (untraced).

1966   Scottie is filmed for a BBC television program.

1970   Scottie's painting *Bird Song* is selected as an image for a UNICEF Christmas card.

1972   Scottie Wilson dies of cancer in London on March 26, at the age of eighty-one.

Exhibition History

The following is what we believe to be a comprehensive list of exhibitions of Scottie
Wilson's work during his lifetime and selected major exhibitions in which his work was
shown posthumously. This information has been compiled from news articles,
information in the Musgrave Kinley Outsider Archive (London), and exhibition
histories published in George Melly, *It's All Writ Out for You: The Life and Work of Scottie Wilson*
(London: Thames and Hudson, 1986), and Helen Marzolf, *Scottie Wilson: The Canadian
Drawings* (Regina, Saskatchewan: Dunlop Art Gallery, 1989).

Self-promoted solo exhibitions are indicated by a dagger (†).
Other solo exhibitions are indicated by an asterisk (*).

1943   *Fantastic Designs by "Scottie,"* Picture Loan Society, Toronto
†980 Granville Street, Vancouver
*Vancouver Art Gallery, Vancouver

1944   *Drawings by "Scottie,"* Picture Loan Society, Toronto
†299 St. Paul Street, St. Catharines, Ontario
Twenty-first Annual Exhibition of the Society of Graphic Art, Art Gallery of Toronto

1945   *Thirty Works by "Scottie" Wilson*, Arcade Gallery, London
(organized by the London Gallery)
Dreams and Designs by "Scottie," Picture Loan Society, Toronto
James McLure & Son's Picture Gallery, Glasgow
Twenty-second Annual Exhibition of the Society of Graphic Art, Art Gallery of Toronto

1946   *Barcelona Restaurant, London
        †*350 Works by "Scottie" Wilson*, Newborough, Scarborough

1947   *Exposition internationale du surréalisme*, Galerie Maeght, Paris
        †Gala-Land Amusements, Great Yarmouth

1948   *Three Types of Automatism: Ernst Martin, Paul Paun, Scottie Wilson*,
        London Gallery
        †Oxford Street, London

1949   **Pen and Brush by Scottie Wilson*, Gimpel Fils, London
        **Exhibition of Decorative Panels*, Passedoit Gallery, New York
        L'Art Brut préféré aux arts culturels, Galerie Drouin, Paris

1950   *Gimpel Fils, London
        "Scottie" Wilson and Denis Williams, Gimpel Fils, London

1951   *Gimpel Fils, London
        *Galerie Nina Dausset, Paris

1952   *Galerie Joos Hutter, Basel
        *Gimpel Fils, London
        **The Aubusson Tapestry by Scottie Wilson*, Galerie de France, Paris
        Phantastische Kunst, XX Jahrhunderts, Kunsthalle, Basel
        Tendances de la peinture et de la sculpture britanniques contemporaines,
        Galerie de France, Paris

1953   **Scottie Wilson Primitives*, Victoria Arts Center, Victoria, British Columbia; Vancouver Art
        Gallery; Regina Public Library, Regina, Saskatchewan; Coste House, Calgary, Alberta;
        Brandon Art Center, Brandon, Manitoba

1955   †The Bookshop, St. Ives

1956   Newport Borough Museum, Newport, South Wales
        **Scottie Wilson: Thirty Recent Works*, Clock Room, David Morgan Limited,
        The Hayes, Cardiff
        †Pontypool Educational Settlement, Monmouthshire

1957   Robertson Galleries, Ottawa

1958   *Colour Drawings by Scottie Wilson*, Picture Loan Society, Toronto
Drawings by Scottie Wilson, Durlacher Brothers, New York
†Battersea

1960   †14/15 Marine Parade, Margate

1962   *Ben Uri Gallery, London

1963   Gallery One, London

1964   *Surrealism in Canadian Painting*, London Public Library, London, Ontario

1966   *Brook Street Gallery, London

1967   *New Charing Cross Gallery, London
*Brook Street Gallery, London
Three Naive Painters: Scottie Wilson, Margaret Baird, Gladys Hamilton Cooper, Moyan Gallery, Manchester
International Exhibition of Naive Painting, Circle Gallery, London
L'Art Brut: Selections de la Collection de l'Art Brut, Musée des Arts Décoratifs, Paris
Irreguliers de l'art, Maison de la Culture, Rennes
Some Paintings, Drawings, and Prints from the Douglas Duncan Collection,
Willistead Art Gallery, Windsor, Ontario

1968   *Old and New Images by Scottie Wilson*, Circle Paintings and Sculpture, London

1969   *Circle Paintings and Sculpture, London

1971   *Scottie Wilson: Drawings and Ceramics*, Ben Uri Gallery, London
Gift from the Douglas M. Duncan and the Milne-Duncan Bequest: An Exhibition at the National Gallery of Canada, National Gallery of Canada, Ottawa

1972   *Third Anniversary Exhibition: The Edmonton Art Gallery*, Edmonton Art Gallery, Edmonton, Alberta

1974   *People's Art: Naive Art in Canada*, National Gallery of Canada, Ottawa

1975   *Margaret Fischer, London
*Gimpel Fils, London

1977   *Warehouse Gallery, London
*Fieldbourne Galleries, London

1978   *Collection de l'Art Brut, Lausanne
        Collection de l'Art Brut, Château de Beaulieu, Lausanne
        Summer 1978, Mercury Gallery, London
        Dada and Surrealism Revisited, Hayward Gallery, London

1979   *Galerie Schreiner, Basel
        Britain's First International Naive Art Exhibition, Hamilton Fine Art, London
        Outsiders, Arts Council of Great Britain, Hayward Gallery, London; Louisiana
        Museum, Humlebaek, Denmark
        Outsiders, Konsten, Liljevalchs Konsthall, Stockholm

1980   *The Penrose Collection of Works by Scottie Wilson*, Mayor Gallery, London
        Their Way: An Exhibition of Four Painters: Scottie Wilson, Alf O'Brian, Nicholas Evans, Ken Watts,
        Bede Gallery, Jarrow, Tyneside
        Wahn oder Wirklichkeit, Galerie Charlotte für naive Kunst, Munich
        Art House, Stockwell London

1981   *The Fantastic Art of Scottie Wilson*, Scottish Gallery, Edinburgh
        XVI Bienal de São Paulo, São Paulo, Brazil
        Paris–Paris, Centre National de l'Art Moderne, Pompidou Centre, Paris

1982   *Two British Primitives: Alfred Wallis and Scottie Wilson*, Mercury Gallery, London
        Aftermath, Barbican Gallery, London
        Scottie Wilson, 1890–1972: Exhibition of Pen Drawings and Watercolours,
        Theo Waddington Galleries, Toronto

1983   *Ascher Textiles*, Redfern Gallery, London

1984   *English Contrasts: Peintures et sculpteurs anglais, 1950–1960*, Artcurial, Paris

1986   *It's All Writ Out for You: The Work of Scottie Wilson, 1888–1972*, Third Eye Centre, Glasgow
        An Exhibition in Memory of Victor Musgrave (1919–1984) by Scottie Wilson (1888–1952 [sic]),
        Mayor Gallery, London
        A Private Paradise: Paintings by Scottie Wilson, Gillian Jason Gallery, London
        *Outsider Archive, London
        *Picturebrokers Gallery, London
        *Galerie "Art en marge," Brussels
        Scottie Wilson (1888–1972): Oeuvres de 1930 à 1946 de L'Ancienne Collection R. Penrose,
        Galerie Messine-Thomas Le Guillou, Paris
        European Outsiders, Rosa Esman Gallery, New York
        Outsiders: Art beyond the Norms, Rosa Esman Gallery, New York

Continent abstrait / Continent surréaliste: Peintres–dessins–collages–object–photographies, Galerie 1900–2000, Paris

1987–88   *In Another World: Outsider Art from Europe and America,* Cornerhouse, Manchester

1989–90   **Scottie Wilson: The Canadian Drawings,* Dunlop Art Gallery, Regina, Saskatchewan; Hart House, University of Toronto; Art Gallery of Windsor, Windsor, Ontario; Mount Saint Vincent University Art Gallery, Halifax, Nova Scotia; Mendel Art Gallery, Saskatoon, Saskatchewan; Southern Alberta Art Gallery, Lethbridge

1992–93   *Parallel Visions: Modern Artists and Outsider Art,* Los Angeles County Museum of Art; Museo Nacional Reina Sofia, Madrid; Kunsthalle Basel; Setagaya Art Museum, Tokyo

1993–95   *Driven to Create: The Anthony Petullo Collection of Self-Taught and Outsider Art,* Museum of American Folk Art, New York; Milwaukee Art Museum; Krannert Art Museum, University of Illinois at Urbana-Champaign; Akron Art Museum; Tampa Museum of Art

1998   *Art Unsolved: The Musgrave Kinley Collection,* Irish Museum of Art, Dublin

1998–99   *Private Worlds: Classic Outsider Art from Europe,* Katonah Museum of Art, New York

1999   *A Collection in the Making,* Irish Museum of Modern Art, Dublin

2000   *Roscrea,* Damer House, Ireland

2000–2001   *ABCD: A Collection of Art Brut,* John Michael Kohler Arts Center, Sheboygan, Wisconsin

2002   *Outsider Art from the Musgrave Kinley Outsider Collection,* Whitworth Gallery, Manchester
Les Chemins de l'Art Brut (1), Musée d'Art Moderne Lille Métropole, Villneuve d'Ascq, France

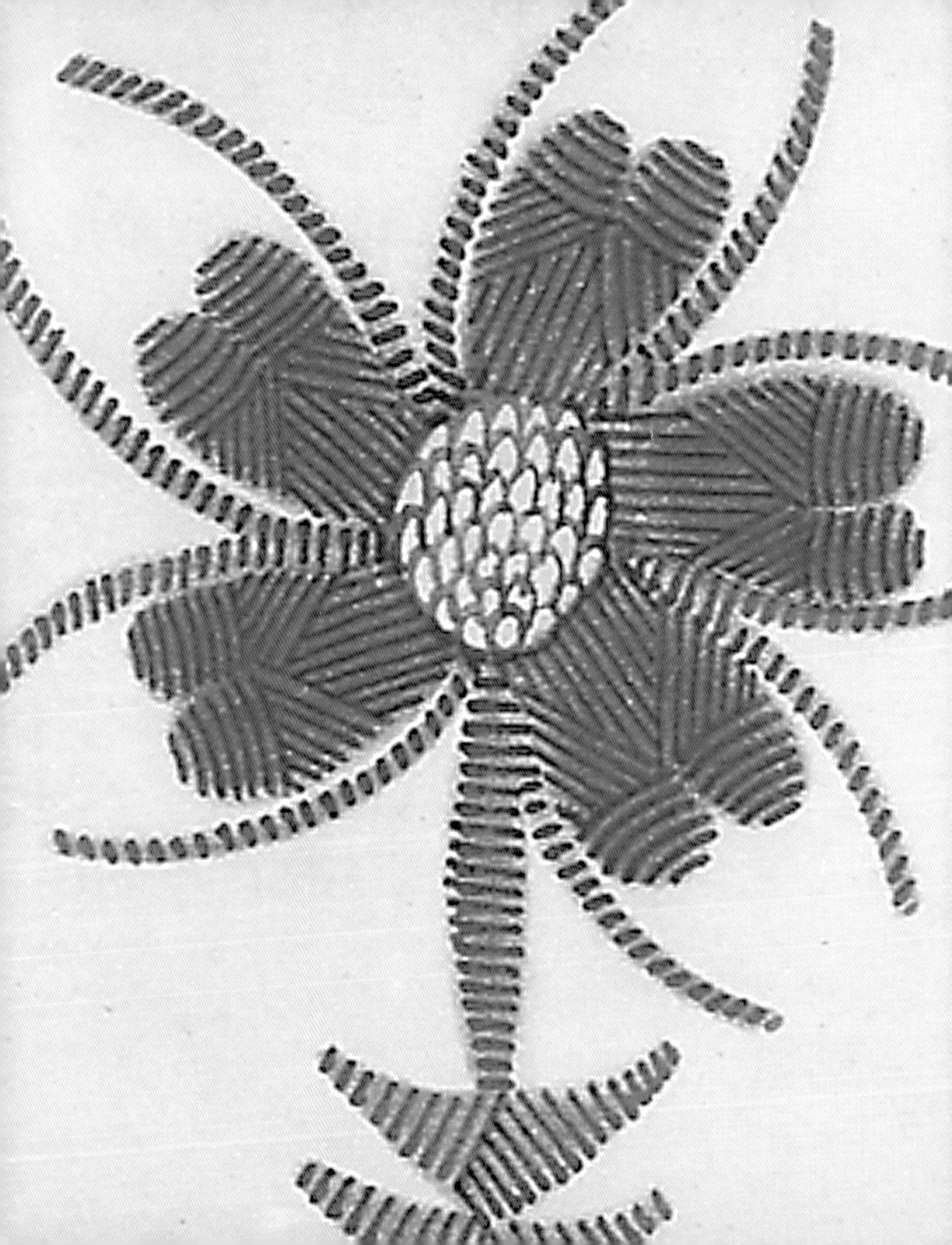

Bibliography

Books

Beardsley, John, and Roger Cardinal. *Private Worlds: Classic Outsider Art from Europe.*
Katonah, N.Y.: Katonah Museum of Art, 1998.

Bihalji-Merin, Oto. *Modern Primitives: Masters of Naive Painting.* London:
Thames and Hudson, 1959.

Cardinal, Roger. "The Art of Scottie Wilson." In *Scottie Wilson.* London: Picturebrokers, 1986.

———. *Outsider Art.* London: Studio Vista, 1972.

England, Jane. *Outsiders & Co.* London: Phaidon, 1996.

Lister, Eric, and Sheldon Williams. *Twentieth-Century British Naive and Primitive Artists.*
London: Astral Books, 1977.

Levy, Mervyn. *Scottie Wilson.* London: Brook Street Gallery, 1966.

Maizels, John. *Raw Creation: Outsider Art and Beyond.* London: Phaidon, 1996.

Marzolf, Helen. *Scottie Wilson: The Canadian Drawings.* Regina, Saskatchewan:
Dunlop Art Gallery, 1989.

Melly, George. *It's All Writ Out for You: The Life and Work of Scottie Wilson.* London:
Thames and Hudson, 1986.

———. *A Tribe of One: Great Naïve Painters of the British Isles.* Oxford: Oxford Illustrated Press, 1981.

Petullo, Anthony. *Self-Taught and Outsider Art: The Anthony Petullo Collection.* Introduction by Jane
Kallir; selected bibliography by Margaret Andera. Urbana: University of Illinois Press, 2001.

Orange and Purple Swans, c. 1955–65 (detail of plate 29)

Rhodes, Colin. *Outsider Art: Spontaneous Alternatives*. London: Thames and Hudson, 2000.

——. *Private Worlds: Outsider and Visionary Art*. Riverside, Twickenham, England: Orleans House Gallery, 2001.

Schreiner, Gérard A. *Scottie Wilson*. Rorschach, Switzerland: Zehnder, 1979.

Thévoz, Michel. *Art Brut*. Foreword by Jean Dubuffet. Geneva: Editions d'Art Albert Skira, 1976.

——. *The Art Brut Collection, Lausanne*. Zurich: Swiss Institute for Art Research, 2001.

Tuchman, Maurice, and Carol S. Eliel. *Parallel Visions: Modern Artists and Outsider Art*. Los Angeles: Los Angeles County Museum of Art; Princeton, N.J.: Princeton University Press, 1992.

Articles

Arts, February 20, 1953 (review). Toronto Reference Library, microfiche.

Barnard, Elissa. "Wilson's Doodles Now Decorative Art." *Halifax Mail Star*, January 13, 1990.

Calgary Herald, January 2, 1954 (review).

Cooper, Emmanuel. "The Secret World of Scottie Wilson." *Art and Artists*, no. 234 (March 1986): 13–17.

Cornishman (Penzance), "Artist's Odd Start: Intriguing Show on View at St. Ives," January 13, 1955.

Crichton, Mamie. "Scottie Wilson." *Scottish Field*, July 1974.

Duncan, Douglas. "Drawings by 'Scottie' Wilson." Publicity sheet for exhibition assembled for the Western Canada Art Circuit and shown at the Fine Arts Gallery, University of British Columbia, November 3–21, 1953.

Duval, Paul. "Scottie Is Puzzled Himself by His 'Dreamt-Up' Pictures." *Telegram* (Toronto), February 8, 1958.

Edmonton Museum of Art Bulletin, "Scottie Wilson," April 1956.

Evening Citizen (Glasgow), "Pictures Paid for Meals: Now Glasgow Man Holds Exhibition," October 6, 1948.

Evening Standard (London), "Somnarticulism," October 4, 1948.

Hambleton, Ronald. "Wilson Art Form Goes Back for Years." Letter to the editor, *Toronto Star*, May 17, 1982.

Hume, Christopher. "'Wandering Junk Dealer' Back in Metro." *Toronto Sunday Star*, May 2, 1982.

Lambert, R. S. "Is There Unrecognized Talent?" *Saturday Night* (Toronto) 58 (April 17, 1943).

Les Lettres français, "Birds on a Tree," February 25, 1953.

Levy, Mervyn. "The Artist at Work: Scottie Wilson's Kingdom in Kilburn." *Studio* 163 (June 1962): 226–31.

———. "Scottie Wilson: The Visionary Experience." *Studio International* 172 (November 1966): 244–47.

Marshall, Doug. "Former Toronto Junk Man Wins International Fame." *Ottawa Journal*, May 2, 1963.

McCarthy, Pearl. Review. *Toronto Globe and Mail*, April 17, 1943, Art and Artists sec.

Mesens, E. L. T. "'Scottie' Wilson." *Horizon* 13 (June 1946): 400–402.

Montreal Star, obituary of Scottie Wilson, March 28, 1972.

More, Ian. "Scotland as I See It: Indian Totem Pole Inspired Picture." *Reynolds News and Sunday Citizen* (London), September 23, 1945.

Mullins, Edwin. "Primitive Skill." *Sunday Telegraph* (London), October 16, 1966.

———. "The Visionary of Kilburn." *Weekend Telegraph* (London), October 10, 1966.

Musgrave, Victor. "Erotic Cosmos." *Art and Artists* 9 (October 1974): 6–9.

New Cavalcade, "Art Mart," July 23, 1949.

News Review, "Automatic Painter's Fear," February 26, 1948.

New York Times, "Primitive Artist Shuns the Public," April 2, 1968.

Observer Review, "The Other Wilson," February 9, 1949.

Ottawa Citizen, "Ex-Junk Dealer Draws International Attention," September 21, 1957.

Ottawa Citizen, "Famed 'Primitive' Artist Puts His Dreams on Paper," September 7, 1957.

Ottawa Citizen, "The Mysterious World of Scottie Wilson," March 2, 1968.

Ottawa Journal, "English Artist Shows Unusual Drawings," September 24, 1957.

Regina (Saskatchewan) Leader-Post, "Wilson Drawings Shown at Library," May 18, 1954.

St. Catharines Standard, "One Man Art Show," June 3, 1944.

St. Ives Times, "Pen Pictures: New Style," January 14, 1955.

"Scottie Wilson." *Publications de la Compagnie de l'Art Brut*, fasc. 4 (1965): 5–31.

"Scottie Wilson: Painted Ceramics and Drawings." *Art and Artists*, no. 234 (March 1986): 35–36.

South Wales Argus, "One-Man Art Exhibition at Newport," May 15, 1956.

Sunday Times (London), "Primitive," March 21, 1965.

Sydney Post Record, "Artist Began by Doodling on Toronto Table-Top," October 19, 1949.

Time, "Scottie's World," September 19, 1949.

Toronto Daily Star, "Scottie Wilson, 82. Primitive Artist," March 28, 1972.

Toronto Globe and Mail, review, February 26, 1944.

Toronto Globe and Mail, "Soaring Artist: Scottie Wilson's Reputation Is High, but He Paints China in a London Slum," April 16, 1963.

Toronto Star, "Scottie Wilson Worthy of Interest," May 31, 1982.

Uhthoff, Ina D. D. "Artist's Work Has Different Approach: Dream Pictures by Scottie Wilson Demonstrate His Unusual Vision," *Victoria Colonist*, February 14, 1954.

Underhill, Stuart. "Noted in Britain as Unique Artist, Began in Toronto." Ontario, 1949 (publication title unknown).

Vancouver Province, "Odd Designs Not Appreciated Here: Ex-Vancouverite Art Sensation," October 21, 1949.

Volke, Brian. Review. *Regina (Saskatchewan) Leader-Post*, May 25, 1989.

Waring, David. "Scottie Wilson, L. Petley-Jones, Suzanne Freemont: Gimpel Fils Gallery." *Art News and Review*, September 24, 1949.

Whittet, G. S. "Scottie Wilson." *Studio* 142 (December 1951): 189–90.

Acknowledgments

We are deeply grateful for the assistance of the people who helped us publish this book. Numerous individuals gave generously of the their time, and sometimes incurred personal expense as well, so that we could tell Scottie Wilson's story. We apologize in advance for omitting anyone we should have acknowledged and for any factual errors in our story.

Our research travels took us to Toronto and Ottawa in Canada and to London and Edinburgh in the United Kingdom. The World Wide Web and many generous libraries took us to other places we needed to visit.

We thank our dear friends Alex Gerrard, Margaret Andera, and Roger Cardinal, who offered encouragement and advice at the outset of this project. A very special thank-you to Monika Kinley of the Musgrave Kinley Outsider Collection for sharing the Victor Musgrave archives as well as her time and personal recollections of Scottie Wilson. We are also grateful to Monika Kinley and Roger Cardinal for their insightful reading of the manuscript, and for sharing their valuable advice and suggestions. Scottie Wilson's story is more complete because of their efforts.

Our research could not have been done without the support of some talented professionals, including Larry Pfaff at the E. P. Taylor Research Library and Archives at the Art Gallery of Ontario, Toronto, who was extremely accommodating in making the archive available during an inventory period, and Cindy Campbell at the National Gallery of Canada, Ottawa, who provided assistance with the Douglas Duncan Archive.

Ann Simpson, senior curator of the archive and library at the National Gallery of Modern Art in Edinburgh, graciously allowed access to the Scottie Wilson archives. The information obtained from these archives was invaluable and essential to completing our story. We thank Ms. Simpson and her associate, Logan Sisley, for their patient assistance during the course of our correspondence concerning items in the Scottie Wilson Archive. Additionally, Ms. Simpson put us in contact with Scottie Wilson's friend George Murray. We are deeply appreciative of Mr. Murray's interesting and enlightening recollections of his time spent with Scottie.

Paul and Margery Clarke of 'The First' Gallery, keepers of the Crispin Eurich archive, were always enthusiastic in their correspondence, more than helpful in their efforts, and most generous in their willingness to make accessible the photos of Scottie that were taken by Eurich, a noted photographer whose pictures of artists are widely respected. We wish them well as they continue to preserve his work and make it accessible for a new generation. Our appreciation also goes to photographer Paul Carter and his staff for facilitating the digital imaging and transfer of the photos from the Crispin Eurich archive for use in our book.

Bill Tilley, historian for the first battalion Cameronians, provided information on Scottie Wilson's time in the Scottish Rifles. Researcher Sue Chestney helped with Freeman family research. Lucy Farrow, assistant archivist at British Telecom, assisted in searching for London telephone records for Scottie. Roy Wild, longtime London taxi driver, was an excellent guide to 37 Lynton Road and many other places where Scottie may have worked or lived. And Liz Crosland, current owner of 37 Lynton Road, provided her insight into Scottie's time at this address.

We wish to thank all of the staff members at the following institutions who personally assisted us in searching archives and libraries: the National Art Library at the Victoria and Albert Museum, London; the Tate Museum Gallery Archives, London; the Scottish National Gallery of Modern Art, Edinburgh; the London Family Records Center; the General Register Office for Scotland, Edinburgh; and the Toronto Reference Library.

We cannot fail to mention the people who have helped us through their correspondence, sharing information that pieced together the Scottie Wilson story. The contributions of these individuals have been extremely important to this project: Anne Blackwood of the Demographic Dissemination Branch at the General Register Office, Scotland; Lynn Brockington, librarian, Vancouver Art Gallery; Joyce Clark at the Dunlop Art Gallery, Regina, Saskatchewan; Riann Coulter, fellow in outsider art at the Irish Museum of Modern Art, Dublin; Christine Garrett, who provided expert translation skills; Stephanie Fawcett, sales executive, Victoria and Albert Images; Gillian Jason of the Gillian Jason Gallery, London; Evelyn Peters McLellan, archivist, City of Vancouver Archives; Charlotte Samuels, assistant curator of furniture, textiles, and fashion at the Victoria and Albert Museum; Megan Schlase at the City of Vancouver Archives; Eva White, Archive of Art and Design, Victoria and Albert Museum.

We would also like to thank Helen Marzolf and George Melly for their correspondence during the writing of this book. Their previous research and writing have provided an exceptional foundation for our study of Scottie's life and work.

And, finally, our thanks to the people who helped bring this book to life: our marvelous editor, Karen Jacobson; our very talented designer, Michelle Pietrzak-Wegner; Kathleen Preciado, who meticulously prepared our index; our longtime and always dependable photographer, Larry Sanders; skilled conservationist Jim DeYoung; and expert printer Friesens Corporation.

Index

Aberdeen
    exhibition, 37–38, *39*
anti-Semitism, 7, 25, 26, 54n. 13
Arcade Gallery, London, 34
    Thirty Works by "Scottie" Wilson, 63
Art brut, 38, 42, 62
    ABCD: A Collection of Art Brut, 67
    L'art brut préféré aux arts culturels, 64
    L'art brut: Selections de la Collection de l'art brut, 65
    Les chemins de l'art brut (1), 67
    Collection de l'art brut, Lausanne, 38, 66
Artcurial, Paris
    English Contrasts: Peintures et sculpteurs anglais, 1950–1960, 66
Art Gallery of Toronto
    Twenty-first Annual Exhibition of the Society of Graphic Art, 29, 63
    Twenty-second Annual Exhibition of the Society of Graphic Art, 63
Art House, London, 66
Arts Council of Great Britain
    Outsiders, 66
Ascher Textiles, 45, 62, 66
"Auxies," 15. *See also* Black and Tans

Baker, Robert, 45
Barbican Gallery, London
    Aftermath, 66
Barcelona Restaurant, London, 34, 64
BBC television program, 46, 62
Bede Gallery, Jarrow
    Their Way: An Exhibition of Four Painters: Scottie Wilson, Alf O'Brian, Nicholas Evans, Ken Watts, 66
Ben Uri Gallery, London, 44, 55, 58n. 110; 62
    Jewish Artists of Great Britain, 44
    Scottie Wilson: Drawings and Ceramics, 65
Black and Tans, 14–15, 25, 61
Blackpool, 38

Blake, William, 41
Breton, André, 38
Brook Street Gallery, London, 65
Burns, Robert, 41

Cameron, Richard, 13
Cameronians (Scottish Rifles), 13, 61
Canada. *See also* Federation of Canadian Artists; Saint
        Catharines; Toronto; Vancouver; Winnipeg
    artist in, 31–32, 55n. 50; 61
    emigration to, 7, 14, 17, 25, 61
    peddler in, 15, 19, 61
Cardinal, Roger, 37, 38, 57n. 86; 73
Centre National de l'Art Moderne, Paris
    Paris—Paris, 66
Chaplin, Charlie, 41
Churchill, Winston, 15
Circle Gallery, London
    International Exhibition of Naive Painting, 65
Circle Paintings and Sculpture, London
    Old and New Images by Scottie Wilson, 65
Clock Room, Cardiff
    Scottie Wilson: Thirty Recent Works, 64
Collection de l'art brut, Lausanne, 38, 66
Cornerhouse, Manchester
    In Another World: Outsider Art from Europe and America, 67
Crichton, Mamie, 10, 22, 58n. 120

Damer House, Ireland
    Roscrea, 67
Dubuffet, Jean, 38, 42, *43*, 62
Duncan, Douglas, 20, 26, 27–28, 33, 40, 55n. 50; 62
    Drawings by "Scottie" Wilson, 56n. 71
    Gift from the Douglas M. Duncan and the Milne—Duncan Bequest, 65
    inventory of Wilson's drawings, 29, 31, 32, 57n. 75

letter to Wilson, 31–32
Some Paintings, Drawings, and Prints from the Douglas Duncan Collection, 65
Dunlop Art Gallery, Regina, Saskatchewan
Scottie Wilson: The Canadian Drawings, 67
Durlacher Brothers, New York
Drawings by Scottie Wilson, 65
Duval, Paul, 21

Edinburgh Weavers
textile design, 45; *pl. 21*
Edmonton Art Gallery, Alberta
Third Anniversary Exhibition, 65
Eurich, Crispin, 74
photographs by, *2, 6, 8, 18, 20, 80*

Fealdman, Barry, 51
Federation of Canadian Artists, 26, 27, 55n. 50; 62
Fieldbourne Galleries, London, 65
folk art, 38
France, 7, 13–14, 42, 44, 61
Freeman, Alan, 9, 15, 33
Freeman, Lewis, 9. *See also* Louis Freeman; Scottie Wilson
Freeman, Louis, 7, 19, 61. *See also* Lewis Freeman; Scottie Wilson
immigration record, 17
name change, 7, 24, 32
residences, 54nn. 27–28
French, Neal, 45
Freud, Lucian, 33

Galerie "Art en marge," Brussels, 66
Galerie Charlotte für naive Kunst, Munich
Wahn oder Wirklichkeit, 66
Galerie de France, Paris
The Aubusson Tapestry by Scottie Wilson, 64
Tendances de la peinture et de la sculpture britanniques contemporaines, 64
Galerie Drouin, Paris
L'art brut préféré aux arts culturels, 64
Galerie Joos Hutter, Basel, 64
Galerie Messine–Thomas Le Guillou, Paris
Scottie Wilson (1888–1972): Oeuvres de 1930 à 1946 de l'ancienne collection R. Penrose, 66
Galerie Nina Dausset, Paris, 64
Galerie 1900–2000, Paris
Continent abstrait/Continent surréaliste, 67
Galerie Schreiner, Basel, 66
Gallery Maeght, Paris
Exposition internationale du surréalisme, 38, 42, 62, 64
Gillian Jason Gallery, London
A Private Paradise: Paintings by Scottie Wilson, 66
Gimpel, Rene and Kay, 46

Gimpel Fils, London, 37, 65
Pen and Brush by Scottie Wilson, 64
"Scottie" Wilson and Denis Williams, 64
Glasgow
city crest, 42
exhibitions, 33–34, 63, 66
Freeman family in, 9–10, 13, 61
peddler in, 14
Grosse, Irving, 44

Hambleton, Ronald, 24, 27, 55n. 50
Hamilton Fine Art, London
Britain's First International Naive Art Exhibition, 66
Harrison, Martin, 40
Hayward Gallery, London
Dada and Surrealism Revisited, 66
Outsiders, 66
Hopkins, Bill, 40, 42, 62

India, 13, 22
Ireland, 14–15
Irish Museum of Art, Dublin
Art Unsolved: The Musgrave Kinley Collection, 67
A Collection in the Making, 67
Irish Republican Army (IRA), 14–15, 41

James McLure & Son's Picture Gallery, Glasgow, 34, 63
John Michael Kohler Arts Center, Sheboygan
ABCD: A Collection of Art Brut, 67

Kar, Ida
photographs by, *12, 16, 30, 36, 46, 48, 50*
Katonah Museum of Art, New York
Private Worlds: Classic Outside Art from Europe, 67
Keegan, John, 15
Kettle, H. Garnard (Rik), 26, 27, 55n. 50
Kinley, Monika, 49, 73
Art Unsolved: The Musgrave Kinley Collection, 67
Outsider Art from the Musgrave Kinley Outsider Collection, 67
Kunsthalle, Basel
Phantastische Kunst, XX Jahrhunderts, 64

Levy, Mervyn, 49, 51
accounts by, 14, 19, 26, 28, 41, 43, 50
with Wilson, 29
Liljevalchs Konsthall, Stockholm
Outsiders, Konsten, 66
London, 37, 40–41, 43
exhibitions, 34, 37, 40, 63, 64, 65, 66. *See also* Ben Uri Gallery; Gimpel Fils
Freeman family in, 9
peddler in, 7, 14, 15, 17

London Gallery, 34, 40, 63
   Three Types of Automatism: Ernst Martin, Paul Paun, Scottie Wilson, 64
London Public Library, Ontario
   Surrealism in Canadian Painting, 65
Los Angeles County Museum of Art
   Parallel Visions: Modern Artists and Outsider Art, 67

Maison de la culture, Rennes
   Irreguliers de l'art, 65
Margaret Fischer, London, 65
Marshall, Doug, 46, 47
Marzolf, Helen, 24, 40, 57n. 75
Mayor Gallery, London
   An Exhibition in Memory of Victor Musgrave (1919–1984) by Scottie Wilson (1888–1952 [sic]), 66
   The Penrose Collection of Works by Scottie Wilson, 66
McCarthy, Pearl, 28
Melly, George, 14, 26, 40, 46, 54n. 14
Mercury Gallery, London
   Summer 1978, 66
   Two British Primitives: Alfred Wallis and Scottie Wilson, 66
Mesens, E. L. T., 24, 33, 34, 57n. 83
Moyan Gallery, Manchester
   Three Naive Painters: Scottie Wilson, Margaret Baird, Gladys Hamilton Cooper, 65
Musée des arts décoratifs, Paris
   L'art brut: Selections de la Collection de l'art brut, 65
Musée d'art moderne Lille métropole, Villneuve d'Ascq
   Les chemins de l'art brut (1), 67
Museum of American Folk Art, New York
   Driven to Create: The Anthony Petullo Collection of Self-Taught and Outsider Art, 67
Musgrave, Victor, 22, 26, 33, 40, 49
   Art Unsolved: The Musgrave Kinley Collection, 67
   An Exhibition in Memory of Victor Musgrave (1919–1984) by Scottie Wilson (1888–1952 [sic]), 66
   Outsider Art from the Musgrave Kinley Outsider Collection, 67
Myerson, Clifford, 14, 15, 17, 26, 51, 59n. 127

National Gallery of Canada, Ottawa
   Gift from the Douglas M. Duncan and the Milne–Duncan Bequest, 65
   People's Art: Naive Art in Canada, 65
Newborough, Scarborough
   350 Works by "Scottie" Wilson, 64
New Charing Cross Gallery, London, 65

Outsider Archive, London, 66
outsider art, 38, 42, 62

Passedoit Gallery, New York
   Exhibition of Decorative Panels, 64
Picasso, Pablo, 34, 24, 62

Picturebrokers Gallery, London, 66
Picture Hire Society, London, 27
Picture Loan Society, Toronto, 26–28, 31, 32, 49
   Colour Drawings by Scottie Wilson, 29, 65
   Drawings by "Scottie," 63
   Dreams and Designs by "Scottie," 63
   Fantastic Designs by "Scottie," 28

Redfern Gallery, London
   Ascher Textiles, 66
Renzius, Rudy, 24
Robertson Galleries, Ottawa, 64
Rosa Esman Gallery, New York
   European Outsiders, 66
   Outsiders: Art beyond the Norms, 66
Royal Irish Constabulary (RIC), 14–15, 61
Royal Worcester Porcelain Company
   ceramics designs, 45, 62; *pls. 18–20*
Rubenstein, Alan, 51, 59n. 127

Saint Catharines, Ontario, 29, 63
São Paulo
   XVI Bienal de São Paulo, 66
Scottish Gallery, Edinburgh
   The Fantastic Art of Scottie Wilson, 66
Scottish Rifles. See Cameronians
somnarticulism, 43
South Africa, 13, 22, 61
surrealism, 34, 37
Switzerland, 44, 45–46, 62

Theo Waddington Galleries, Toronto
   Scottie Wilson, 1890–1972: Exhibition of Pen Drawings and Watercolours, 66
Third Eye Center, Glasgow
   It's All Writ Out for You: The Work of Scottie Wilson, 1888–1972, 66
Toronto, 19, 25–27, 29, 61
   exhibitions, 63. *See also* Picture Loan Society

Underhill, Stuart, 26
United Nations Children's Fund (UNICEF), 55, 59n. 128; 62

Vancouver, 23, 24, 26, 27, 28
   exhibitions, 29, 63
   Stanley Park, 26, 56n. 60
Vancouver Art Gallery, 29, 63
Victoria Arts Center
   Scottie Wilson Primitives, 64

Warehouse Gallery, London, 65
Waring, David, 44
Waterman Pen Company, 38

Whitworth Gallery, Manchester
  Outsider Art from the Musgrave Kinley Outsider Collection, 67
Willistead Art Gallery, Windsor
  *Some Paintings, Drawings, and Prints from the Douglas Duncan
    Collection*, 65
Wilson, Robert. *See* Scottie Wilson
Wilson, Scottie. *See also* Lewis Freeman; Louis Freeman
  artistic technique, 19–23, 37, 43–44, 45, 46
  education, 9–10, 33, 41, 43
  exhibitions
    gallery, 27–29, 33–34, 37–38, 40, 42, 44–45,
      46, 62, 63–67
    self-promoted, 29, 37–40, 62, 63, 64, 65
  family, 9–10, 22, 33, 50, 53n. 2–4, 7; 61
  imagery, 20–23, 41, 44, 47, 58n. 97
    "evils" and "greedies," 22, 42, 44, 58n. 100
  Jewish heritage, 9, 17, 25–26, 44–45
  name change, 7, 24–25, 32, 38, 55n. 52; 61
  occupations
    lumberjack, 54n. 22
    military and police service, 13–15, 17, 26, 40
    peddler, 7, 10, 14, 15, 17, 19, 24, 26, 32
  personality, 7, 32–33, 37, 40–42, 45–46, 49–51
  relationships with women, 17, 23–24, 26–27
Wilson, Scottie. Photographs of
  by Eurich, *2, 6, 8, 18, 20, 80*
  by Kar, *12, 16, 30, 36, 46, 48, 50*
  with Dubuffet, *43*
  with Levy, *20*
Wilson, Scottie. Works
  Animal and Globe (Atlas Greedy), pl. 5
  Big Blue Butterfly, pl. 32
  Bird Song, 59n. 128; 62
  Black and White with Yellow Windows, pl. 30
  Black Mouse, pl. 2
  Black/Pink Fish and Faces, pl. 9
  Blue Birds in the Tree, pl. 14
  Butterfly Palace II, pl. 31
  Center Fish Circle on Black, cover, pl. 22
  Figure—8 Faces, pl. 11
  Five Butterflies, pl. 24
  Five Circles on Blue, pl. 27
  The Greedies, pl. 1
  Green Brown Greedies, pl. 10
  Herd of Greedies, pl. 4
  Magic Castle in the Mirror, pl. 23
  Orange and Purple Swans, 68; *pl. 29*
  painted plates, 44–45, 46, 62; *pls. 16–20*
  Pinwheel, pl. 6
  Red Fish Blue Fish in Brown Circle, 11; *pl. 25*
  Red Vase, 60; *pl. 26*
  Sailing Totems, pl. 7
  Spring, pl. 13
  Square with Seven Circles, 52; *pl. 12*
  Temple of Light, pl. 8
  textiles, 45, 62; *pl. 21*
  Three Vases, 35; *pl. 28*
  Yellow Birds in the Tree, pl. 15
  Yellow Fish and Faces, pl. 3
Winnipeg, 24, 26, 27, 62
World War I, 13–14, 61

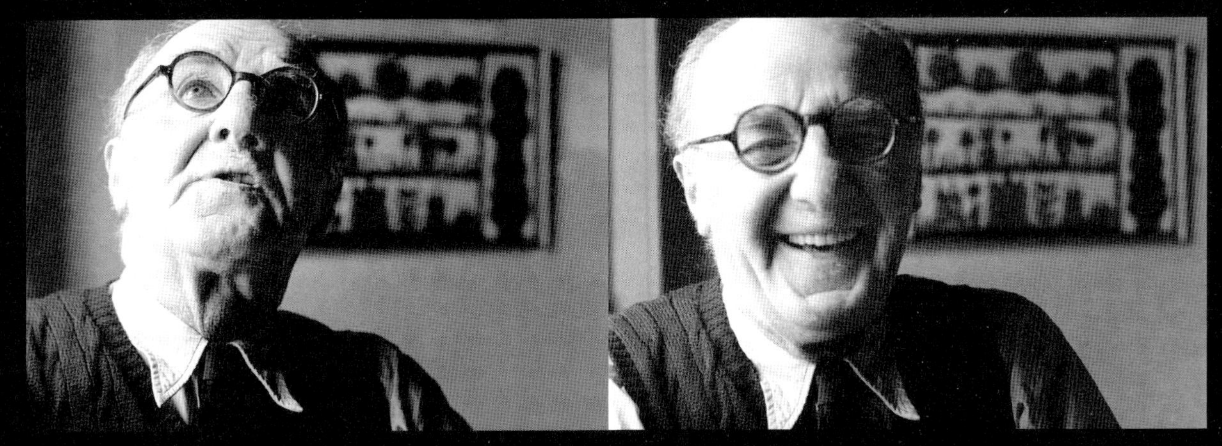

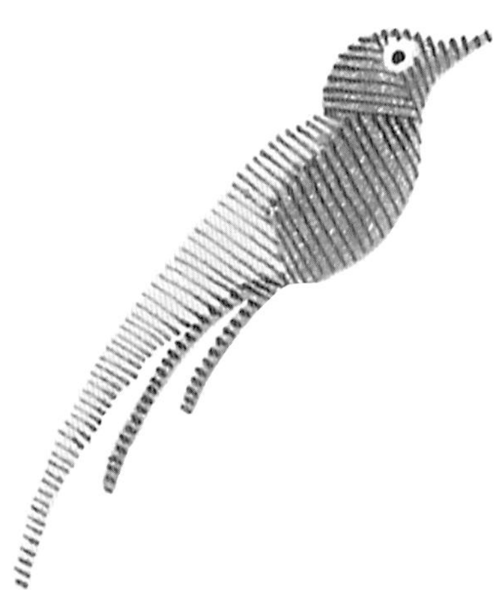